THE SEARCH FOR SELF-RESPECT

Other books by Maxwell Maltz

DR. PYGMALION

ADVENTURES IN STAYING YOUNG

THE PRIVATE LIFE OF DR. PYGMALION

THE MAGIC SCALPEL

THE SECRET OF DR. MCLENAN

A VILLAGE IN FLORENCE

PSYCHO-CYBERNETICS

THE MAGIC POWER OF SELF IMAGE PSYCHOLOGY

CREATIVE LIVING FOR TODAY

THE CONQUEST OF FRUSTRATION

PSYCHO-CYBERNETICS AND SELF-FULFILLMENT

POWER PSYCHO-CYBERNETICS FOR YOUTH

THE SEARCH FOR SELF-RESPECT

by Maxwell Maltz, M.D.

GROSSET & DUNLAP
A National General Company

Publishers
New York

To E. Trine Starnes, Jr.

Library of Congress Catalog Card Number: 72–77095
ISBN: 0–448–01293–6

11-8-73

Third printing

CONTENTS

1. Your Great Need: Self-Respect   3
2. Understanding: The Key to Human Dignity   17
3. The Active Power of Sincerity   33
4. Winning Out Over Uncertainty   48
5. Your Struggle to Overcome Resentment   63
6. Your Third Enemy: Emptiness   83
7. Developing the Strength to Seize Opportunities   97
8. Real Forgiveness: Active Forgiveness   114
9. The Dynamic Potential for Mirror Watchers   131
10. Tear Down Those Prison Walls   146
11. Tranquillity and Self-Respect   162
12. The Active Life: No Retirement Clock   180
13. Integrity as a Way of Life   197
14. Survival with Self-Respect   214
15. Goal Builders   230

58320

THE SEARCH FOR SELF-RESPECT

CHAPTER 1

Your Great Need:
Self-Respect

WHEN you wake up in the morning, throwing off your blankets and blinking the sleep from your eyes, you prepare to meet a curious world.

It is a world of extravagant technological achievement. Skyscrapers thrust themselves heavenward, products of man's ingenuity, up toward the jets that whiz through our skies at speeds no one would have believed thirty years ago. Down below, on our well-built highways, unending processions of gleaming automobiles move forward. All these are products of man's inventive capacities, all reflections of a technological level of accomplishment unknown to the pages of written history before us. Computers aid us in our calculations while the telephone—once a miracle!—pulls us into close communication. Our world is full of elevators and can openers—diesel engines and lawnmowers.

What a world for people today! What a world of overwhelming achievment! There are comforts beyond compare for all the people who wake up in the morning and plunge out of the world of sleep into the world of activity.

And yet it is a world full of people reeling in confusion, trying to find themselves, seeking life's answers, and, in short, searching oh-so-ardently for that inner feeling that is so elusive—self-respect.

For how do you measure the value of a man's life? How do you measure the value of a woman's life? There are so many people in this huge world of yours and mine—how do you measure the value of their lives?

In dollars and cents? In totaling up their bank accounts, their stocks and bonds, their real-estate holdings, their total new worth? In tangible property? Do you take an inventory and assess the accumulations? Automobiles, house, fur coats, diamond rings, television sets, household appliances?

Is this how you take a human being, a creature of God born without his will into this large world of ours, and assess the value of his life? Is this how you place a value on his personal qualities, his skills, his years of experience in living?

Certainly not. Some people might use such yardsticks; I feel they are misguided.

For if there is anything that I have learned in my sixty-five-plus years in this world, if there is anything that has survived the ups and downs of my life, it is this knowledge: *That there is no more accurate measure of an individual's value than his own degree of self-respect.*

And that is why I am writing this book.

More and more I have come to appreciate the great importance of self-respect. As the years have passed following the publication of *Psycho-Cybernetics* (and then *The Magic Power of Self-Image Psychology* and *Creative Living for Today*) I have realized more and more how the nucleus of my ideas on psycho-cybernetics, expressed in these three books, has been the concept of self-respect as a guiding force.

And as I have traveled throughout most of the states of our great country, lecturing to people and talking to them on a one-to-one basis, this realization has become conviction. For on meeting people—young people, senior citizens, church people, irreligious people, rich and poor—I have felt that, regardless of their diverse backgrounds and the uniquely individual character of their experiences, this is what they seek for themselves: self-respect.

People reach out today—in a complicated, changing, and uncertain world—for a sense of their own individual identity. But they don't want just any kind of identity; what they seek is an identity they can be proud of. They want to know who they are, *and* they want to feel a sense of respect for who they are.

We live in a world in which respect for the dollar is considerable, and in which respect for the materialistic products a dollar can buy is also considerable.

Well and good—I like my comforts, too. But how about a more basic emphasis—on respect for one's self? Why is this more basic? Because with self-respect, you reach out toward your full potential as a human being. Because without self-respect, you are a criminal in hiding, living in a prison you have built around yourself, and even if the prison is comfortable and luxurious, it is still a prison.

So this is why I write this book on self-respect. I make no claims that readers of my other books will find it startlingly new in concept because I carry into it ideas I have spent a lifetime developing, some of which are expressed in one form or another elsewhere. I will, of course, draw freely from my many years of experience as a plastic surgeon and, needless to say, I will apply my concepts of psycho-cybernetics to this crucial area of self-respect.

Nevertheless, I do believe that readers old and new will find in these pages both fresh and arresting material to spur and challenge them, and positive, helpful, useful suggestions to aid them in moving toward a good feeling about themselves and their position of dignity and status in the world.

Reaching Out Toward the Best in Yourself

And so let us begin this great search of ours, this search for self-respect.

How do we begin this great process of reaching out toward the best in ourselves? How do we begin this great treasure hunt? First and foremost, by cementing our determination, by feeling strongly about our search.

To reach out only tentatively, timidly, toward the best in yourself is not enough.

To say in yourself, "I have nothing good in me, I know that, but I'll give it a try anyway"—this is not enough.

And to tell yourself, "This is an impossible world, to feel self-respect these days is hopeless, but I'll try to keep an open mind"—this also is not enough.

This is not an easy world to live in. Many people live incomplete lives, bedeviled by the swift pace of change and frustrated by the endless chain of complications, and therefore the search for self-respect is a difficult one. Confusion, pain, despair, dissociation: Millions of people live with these feelings in today's world. Self-respect, success, dignity: These sweeter feelings are harder to come by. To reach them, therefore, you must *will* to reach them. You must feel determined to reach them. You must feel enthusiasm for your goals.

All of us experience, now and then, feelings of boredom, of inertia, of what's the difference. At such times nothing looks good: Steak looks like dogmeat, and when you eat it, it tastes even worse. You look at yourself in the mirror and say to yourself, *"Why does that have to be me?"*

All right; we all get into moods like this. Laugh at them; they're just human. But the important point is this: Your next move is forward, out of this inertia into determination and enthusiasm. For something. For some goal. For some *worthwhile* goal.

My goal in writing this book, your goal in reading this book, must be a determination to find—in you, in me—the self-respect we must feel to lead lives of fulfillment and happiness.

A determination. Not a halfhearted gesture, but a real determination. Nothing else will do.

Let me tell you about the kind of determination I mean. I found it recently when I was lecturing in Detroit.

I was about to address my audience when I noticed a woman helping a man (her husband) walk into the auditorium. He limped along, supported by the woman and by a cane; his leg was in a cast. This startled me somewhat, but I was truly amazed when I saw his clothes; under his overcoat he wore his pajamas. Outside there was snow on the ground and here he came, walking slowly, in his pajamas.

I talked to him, got to know him a little, even had him up on the lecture platform with me. He was, I would estimate, in his late fifties or early sixties. He was interested in my ideas and wanted to hear me speak—and I learned that he had traveled twenty-five miles through the snow to hear me lecture. He had been very eager to come on time—thus the pajamas.

There he stood, leg in cast, pajamas—we were photographed together—and surely this man, though smiling cordially, was the very image of determination. I learned that he was living with half a kidney; that didn't stop him either. Men with two good legs could not move; he, leg in cast, insisted on moving. In terms of determination, he was Babe Ruth out to hit another home run, Joe Louis out after another knockout. What did he want? Self-respect.

During the last couple of years I have done a great deal of lecturing, and I have talked personally to thousands of people.

One, a young man also in the Detroit area, had studied in psycho-cybernetics workshops and was later a teacher for the workshops. What is so unusual about this? The fact that he is blind, that he cannot see—and yet emotionally he sees better than many people who have vision.

Another young man in his twenties decided to teach the inmates of a state penitentiary some of my ideas on more worthwhile living. I was impressed that a man so young, at an age where so many are often limited in their sense of responsibility, could feel so strongly for others that he could reach out even to anti-social people with a real desire to help them.

These young men, too, possess the determination that I refer to—determination to feel respect for themselves and for others.

This is the way you must feel as you start off with me on this journey. You must want to make the most of your life. You must have strong feelings about this conviction and not be ashamed of it—and why should you be? This is your life that is at stake! You should be willing, like that man in Detroit, to travel twenty-five miles through the snow, your leg in a cast, your arm in a cast, your head swathed in bandages, if it will help you just a little bit toward more self-respect.

Not to hear me speak—that is irrelevant—but to reach out toward anything that will help you to feel a greater sense of personal worth.

The Nature of Self-Respect

I have already implied that there is no necessary connection between financial and materialistic success and self-respect. If I have not made my views absolutely clear, let me do so now.

I believe in positive thinking and beyond that to positive imagining and then carrying the entire process forward into successful goal-directed action. I believe in getting out into the world and achieving success in this world—which, with all its imperfections, is the only world we've got.

As a plastic surgeon, I have operated on many famous people, people whose names you would recognize immediately, people who make enormous sums of money through their talents and their positions, people whom the world labeled successes—and yet who regarded themselves as failures. Because they lacked self-respect. Thus there is no necessary correlation between success as the world sees it and self-respect.

Today, after years of writing and lecturing and meeting people and talking to them, this is more clear to me than ever. Worthwhile goals and worthwhile achievements are very important to anyone. Successes are important, too, as is setting goals. Still, the basic feeling of self-respect is something that, initially, you manufacture inside yourself. You have the choice between self-rejection and self-respect; and in the pages of this book we will analyze the very nature of *your feeling* of self-respect from the foundation on up.

As an illustration of what I have been saying, let me tell you about a man I met while on lecture tour. Although by all conventional criteria he was a success, he lacked self-respect and therefore did not enjoy his success.

He was a computer salesman—a top-notch computer salesman. He had been married for a number of years. He had children. He supported his family more than adequately. He had earned the respect of his family and of people in his community. But he hadn't earned his own self-respect. With all his achievements, he could not give himself this feeling.

When he was growing up, his parents had been divorced. The product of a broken home, he had not ever been able to put himself together again to his complete satisfaction.

I talked to this man—he was very likeable, I thought—and gave him some advice that I sincerely hope helped him to feel better about himself, for he deserves his self-esteem.

Our aim in this book is to achieve a kind of self-respect that is real and dependable, that does not hinge on either your financial condition or the state of world affairs, that can weather the disapproval of your neighbors or the anger of your boss at work. This is Self-respect with a capital S, and this, in the final analysis, is the only factor that can make the world inside you go round so that you feel truly secure, regardless of all the external forces which you cannot possibly control.

This is SELF-RESPECT!

Using Your Mind

Self-respect, then, is basically something that you manufacture for yourself in your mind. You must, therefore, learn to use this mind of yours. You know how to use your automobile. You know how to use your television set. Now—and so much more essential to your self-respect as a human being—you must learn how to use your mind.

Let me digress for a moment or two at this point and tell you about my father. Preparing to write this book, I spent an afternoon once just thinking and smoking my cigars, thinking about starting to write a book about self-respect—and I began to think about my father, who had, while he lived, taught me so much about other people and about how to live, and who in so many ways, as most fathers do, helped me to shape my destiny.

My father came to this country from Austria. He was a great designer of clothes and he set up a business in this country as a clothes designer. He was wonderful at using his hands and, in retrospect, I realize how I gravitated toward the field of plastic surgery which, of course, also requires deft, skillful hands.

My father was a very religious man and he always tried to apply his ethical principles to people in a practical way. In our community on New York's Lower East Side, where I grew up, more than once I saw him arbitrate a dispute among neighbors, or perhaps break up a brewing fistfight between two of the hotter young bloods out to prove their manhood.

He believed strongly in giving people a square deal, and he never failed to return a favor or to give people the benefit of their good intentions—even if these intentions were not obvious on the surface. And he prided himself on his sense of self-respect. He nurtured it as one would a flower by placing it in the sun to flourish. He lived for his sense of self-respect —the feeling that he was a worthwhile, positive person— and he worked to develop it.

I remember once—I was very young, not yet even a teenager—and I went to his place of business, where people were working with the cloth that was an essential in his life. It was early in the afternoon and the workers had just returned from lunch. One man handled the cloth with greasy fingers; my father saw him do this and became enraged. Grease on his cloth! On his cloth! He felt his artistry being sullied, his goodness being dirtied. Dad had a violent temper, and he started toward the irresponsible laborer, hand raised, ready to strike him in his sudden wrath.

It hurt him that his rage would overcome him like this, and he started away from the man, mortified, his sense of self-respect endangered, and walked into his own private office to sit there quietly until he could control his anger. Then, restored, he returned to tell the man calmly and quietly not to soil the cloth.

I have always remembered this—how upset he had been, and how he had retreated in order to advance toward his sense of self-respect.

At home, too, my father, usually friendly and agreeable, would sometimes find himself threatened by his temper. One of my brothers or sisters would do something to outrage him and, in a flash, his hand would be raised to spank the offender. He didn't like this in himself, he would draw back his hand and retreat to a little room where he could be by himself— his bedroom or the kitchen, perhaps. When he came back his sense of self-respect would be restored; he would have kind words for the children and a friendly smile for everybody.

There were, as you can see, two sides to my father, and he battled mightily to win this fight with himself—self-respect would win.

Many years later—after my father died in a tragic, sudden accident—I remembered my father's habit and incorporated it into my theories of psycho-cybernetics. You can do yourself a good turn and give yourself relaxation from your tensions if, instead of plunging headlong and heedless into a difficult and frustrating situation, you go to rest for a while—in a quiet room in your mind where you can be alone. Think, refresh yourself and prepare once more to go out and meet life's battles head-on with your self-respect restored.

But, to return to my point, you must learn to use your mind to develop your sense of self-respect, and in the pages of this book we will examine ways in which you can do this. For as it was in his mind that my father was able to quiet his surging emotions and restore to himself his dignity, so must you —in your way, with your special problems, with your unique assets and liabilities—give yourself your self-respect.

In your mind.

Where good things start.

Finding the Self You Like

We hear a great deal about identity problems these days. We hear about millions of people caught in an over-mechanized and impersonal society, losing themselves in the midst of the vastness and the impersonality. And, truth to tell, we live in a world that is growing and growing. One billion people in 1830, two billion in 1930, three billion in 1960— experts predict a world population of seven and one-half billion by the year 2000, and a population of three hundred million in the United States before 2000.

How do you keep firm hold on your identity in such a huge world? How do you feel the importance of *yourself* as a human being?

Studies have shown that teenagers growing up into adult-

hood in this world underrate themselves. Adults, according to this study, consider teenagers more worthy than the teenagers consider themselves.

As for adults, their dissatisfaction with themselves is reflected in rising incidence of alcoholism, of divorce, and of an increasing cynicism about whether or not there is real meaning in life.

Some people seek identity in the way they clothe themselves, and old-fashioned people, used to conventional manners of dress, easily are startled when they go out into the streets and see identity-seeking people parading around in down-to-the ground overcoats, up-to-the-thigh skirts, peekaboo dresses, and plunging necklines—and, that's not all, with outlandish hair, makeup and so on.

Many people seek to find themselves through promiscuous sex, but does it work? I doubt it. Studies have shown that promiscuous women gain little sexual satisfaction from their adventures and that promiscuous men have difficulty relating to other people. It is also interesting to note that research has shown that call girls—glamour figures of today to some people—lack the capacity to establish wholesome, worthwhile interpersonal relationships.

And so people—struggling people, seeking to do something with their lives—earnestly reach out for identity for themselves. In conventional ways. In unconventional ways.

But the question is, or should be, *What kind of identity?* For you can come to grips with what you are, you can *identify* yourself, but still not like what you are.

So you have to do more than find an identity for yourself. You have to build a sense of self that you like. To live the good life, you have to learn how to give yourself something of priceless value—self-respect.

That is what we will think about in this book—how you can build inside yourself a sense of self-respect, of dignity as a human being, that you can feel secure with.

These are not hollow words. Self-respect is our great need today. Obviously we live with materialistic plenty and super-plenty. All you have to do is go shopping in a department store or supermarket and you can see this. Or, if you read the financial section of your daily newspaper, chances are you know the indexes are going up.

Prosperity is not around the corner, but here and now. Still, what good is this prosperity if you don't *feel* prosperous? Affluence. A chicken in every pot is Depression talk; today the talk is about two cars in every garage. Still, you are as affluent as you feel you are. There is a character in an O. Henry short story who feels affluent when she has potatoes, beef, and onions—even though penniless. On the other hand, if you don't feel the inner assurance of your respect for yourself, you can earn an income in six figures and still feel impoverished.

What is the great, crying need of people today? Prosperity is not enough; affluence is not enough. A sense of full, dependable self-reliance is needed—the supporting feeling that they respect themselves.

We will do more than treat self-respect as an intellectual concept or a vague verbal formulation. In accordance with my theories of psycho-cybernetics, we will set practical goals that we can accomplish.

I hope that you will not be lazy in reading this book, but that you will try to turn ideas into practice, so that you can truly reactivate the functioning of your success mechanism. Learn to use your imagination constructively, and help yourself in an active, responsible way toward respectfulness toward yourself—as you are—as an individual and as you function in your world.

"Nothing is good, I see, without respect." William Shakespeare wrote this hundreds of years ago and, as so many of his lines, this one lives in the present as well as in the past and in the future. For our purposes, let's amend *respect* to *self-respect*; and then let us start our search for self-respect.

CHAPTER 2

Understanding:
The Key to Human Dignity

AND so we are off on our mission: We seek the keys to unlock the treasure chest of our sense of self-respect. We seek to find, to recapture, to reinvigorate our human dignity.

Our weapons are invisible but potent. Understanding is one of our key weapons. For to live fruitfully in a subtle civilized society in which complexities are not always spelled out for us, in which we must often seek beneath superficial appearances to discover truth and to differentiate reality from fantasy, we must be understanding people. We must understand ourselves—complex people that we are—and we must understand other people, even while they may hide the essence of their personalities behind various affectations and poses.

And, in truth, we must accomplish not one, but two, tasks. We must become more understanding and, at the same time, we must become less *mis*understanding. Anatole France was a writer who believed there was great misunderstanding in the world. He thought that the development of just a little understanding was a far greater achievement than building one's life on the quicksand of many and monumental misunderstandings.

We read volumes and volumes on the nature of racial and religious prejudice these days—and yet is not prejudice, in its essence, misunderstanding?

A recent study of Catholic schools showed that 53 percent of the students had unfavorable opinions of Jews and 33 percent thought ill of Negroes. But what caliber of understanding was behind these opinions? What experience with Negroes or Jews are they based on—if any?

A poll on anti-Semitism in France indicated that half the population was opposed to the idea of a Jewish president, one-third was against Jewish representatives in government, and one-fifth would not consult a Jewish doctor (they feared poisoning, mostly). Misunderstanding running wild.

What is even more shocking, perhaps, is that in a study of 505 American country clubs 498 indicated that they were opposed to accepting Jewish members.

These studies, these polls, were made quite recently. We hear often—and with good reason—these days of the many abuses inflicted on Negro people because of irrational prejudice and misunderstanding, so much that this needs no documenting; but the misunderstanding rampant in the world spreads out in many directions and the ignorance behind all these misunderstandings is truly staggering. It is especially interesting to note that, as regards the poll on anti-Semitism in France, researchers found the strongest prejudice in communities with no Jews.

I don't bring these studies up to write about the problems of these two minority groups; although it is interesting that the Catholics, who are prejudiced against others today, have been the object of prejudice themselves—that none had been elected president of the United States until just a few years ago. My main purpose in mentioning all this, nevertheless, is to write about the enormous human problem of misunderstanding, a global problem of almost unbelievable dimensions. We must become more understanding, less *mis*understanding individuals if we would aspire to make the world—and our internal world—a better place to live in.

And thus we reach out, attempting to reach full awareness, toward our full self-respect as human beings, judging ourselves charitably, coming to grips with our true personalities, appreciating ourselves with friendship, and then reaching out toward others not with animosity or prejudice but with the same helping hand of friendship and of constructive intentions.

This is no easy thing to do. We are more likely to misunderstand than to understand ourselves and other people. In truth, this may be a protective phenomenon in which we defend ourselves against possible enemies; thus we may come to use misunderstanding as protective armor, but it leads to more misunderstanding and the setting up of a vicious cycle in which you just can't win.

Misunderstanding as a Way of Life

More on misunderstanding. Why? Because it is so prevalent—over the world, over our great nation, among all age groups, among all income groups, among children and among senior citizens. Before we can erect our great structure of self-respect, we must select the site and clear the foundation of debris—and the debris obstructing the building of *understanding* is *misunderstanding*.

When I was a young "tough guy," everybody misunderstood everybody. We had lots of gang fights on New York's Lower East Side. We had them every day sometimes. We teenaged terrors clustered in gangs and warred on each other. We armed ourselves with sticks (from stickball), broken bottles, and bricks. For protective shields to ward off the blows of the bloodthirsty foe, we took the tops of old-fashioned wash-kettles that the women used to wash clothes in in those days.

Thus the young bloods of one block would come to visit— and it was not exactly love thy neighbor. The two gangs would clash, *boom!*

How did the fights start? It was pride that did it—stubborn pride. A member of one gang would seem to "affront" a member of the other gang, the little misunderstanding would become a grudge, the grudge would become a mortal injury, and. . . . You know the rest—bricks, bats, sticks, stones, wash-kettle tops. The adults would rush into stores and apartment buildings to take shelter and we kids would smash each other around until the police came rushing to the rescue.

It was Armageddon; D-day; Custer's Last Stand! From tenement roofs the neighborhood snipers crouched with beebee guns, and the marksmanship was superb. When finally the fighting was over, usually no one even remembered how it started! Yet someone was usually hurt, and occasionally wagons came to cart away the most seriously injured to the hospital.

It is true that it could have been worse—I understand that in more recent times, teenage "rumbles" with switchblades have resulted in deaths; whereas our gang fights never, to my knowledge, ended in anything so tragic and final.

Still, ours were bad enough. To a degree, of course, they stemmed from overflowing teenage energy and from aggression seeking an outlet. But they also stemmed from an appalling lack of communication between people—then as today.

For today we still find ourselves in a chaotic world where adults, not teenagers, cannot seem to communicate with and understand each other. Witness: Suspicion among the Great Powers; race riots in American cities; rising crime rate; rising divorce rate; and alcoholism as a way of life. These are among the leading symptoms of twentieth-century life, and they spell out an inability of people to accommodate themselves to each other.

In 1968, I was lecturing in Washington to about eight hundred executives of insurance companies. At that time Washington was aflame with violence, riots, and looting—products of centuries of misunderstanding. A fundamental human right had been abridged: That one person is as good as another and that we are all children of God, born with rights to happiness and to the feeling that we are human beings of dignity.

The police rushed out in force to cope with the situation, and eventually they restored order to our nation's capital.

Still, police are no answer to the worldwide problem of misunderstanding. We do not have enough police to stop all the inner and outer riots in all the streets and highways and byways of the world. We do not have enough police to stop all the violence and resentful fury of the world's teeming population. There are never enough police; and there never can be enough police.

The victory of understanding over misunderstanding starts

when you police yourself first. It starts when you take charge of the riot inside you and when you police the potential fires of violence before they erupt. It starts when you come to terms with your anti-social impulses and police them properly, channeling them into healthy, aggressive, goal-directed outlets.

By "policing yourself" I do not mean that you put yourself in jail. Nor do I mean that you emotionally imprison yourself. My concept of understanding is this:

1. You seek to identify your needs, and to work toward their realization.

2. You try to find out who you are in relation to other people.

3. You understand that there is greatness in yourself, that there is greatness in other people, that there is indeed greatness in all people.

You don't have to be a hero to be great. Your name doesn't have to be Franklin D. Roosevelt or John F. Kennedy or Dwight Eisenhower; it doesn't have to be a name anyone outside your family recognizes at all. Your greatness comes from your recognition of the best in yourself, from the human dignity that you give yourself, from the sense of self-respect that is your present to yourself from yourself every day of the year —not just on Christmas.

This is how you police yourself in a kindly spirit so as to lead yourself away from misunderstanding as a way of life and redirect yourself towards real self-commitment. When you do this, you are free and you are on the road to self-respect.

The Power of Understanding

When you understand yourself, when you understand others, you are a powerhouse. You hold the trump cards. Because you are honest with yourself, no one can trump you, and no one can stump you.

Still, to misunderstand is easy. To understand is more difficult.

Our news media headline the "generation gap," but what is this but a much-publicized series of misunderstandings between young people today and their elders? I can't help but wonder why there should be such a "gap." I'm over sixty-five years old and I think I get along pretty well with teenagers—and, at the same time, I understand the different perspectives with which older people look out at the world. Why can't everybody bridge this "gap" between the generations and accept the fact that people differ and times change and values do not remain static?

I know a middle-aged woman who is very unhappy because her daughter—married and with a young baby—will not tolerate her in her home. The older woman is attractive and lives in one of the wealthier communities in Connecticut on a thirty-acre estate with tennis courts, swimming pool, bridle path—the American Dream.

Yet she cries to herself because her daughter has so completely rejected her. Sometimes she telephones and knows the daughter is home, but the daughter does not answer the ringing if she thinks it is her mother. When the mother offers to come over to help with the grandchild or to baby-sit, the daughter always turns her down flat.

Now life is often like tennis—it goes two ways, back and forth—and there is a reason for the daughter's total rejection.

I know about it. The mother was too domineering when the daughter was young; she was so bossy then that the daughter still defends herself by keeping her away. This gap is even wider than the generation that stands between the two. Oceans separate mother and daughter. Misunderstandings keep them gulfs apart, stranger than strangers to each other. The mother keeps trying to bridge the gap; the daughter keeps rejecting—rigidly cold, chillingly polite.

The mother has erred; but does not the daughter err still more, in refusing to make the smallest concession, in refusing to take the tiniest step toward even a token reconciliation in the name of forgiveness of human error and attempted understanding?

Anybody can misunderstand; anybody can turn their grievances into lifetime grudges. The person who concentrates on building his own sense of human dignity, and who also insists on human dignity and sincerely tendered understanding for other people is the exceptional person.

The daughter in this case lacked understanding—both of herself and of her mother. She did not realize that she was no longer a little girl, that her mother could no longer dominate her. She did not grasp the reality that she had nothing to fear, that she need not flinch from the forceful nature of the mother's personality. Moreover, she did not see her mother—then or now—with sensitive, understanding eyes, empathizing with the difficulties she had lived through in her lifetime, feeling for her conflicts and her problems and her ups and her downs, the human imperfections of a woman, not a goddess.

The daughter—it is not easy for her to understand, for deep scars are painful—but I feel that she must if she is to make peace with herself. She must have compassion for herself and for her mother as well. Perhaps she will never feel close to her mother, but she must try to understand.

Now let me tell you about two other people—more fortunate people in that they are closer to their need to understand themselves and other people.

One is in a most unglamorous occupation—she is an elevator operator in the building where I live and work when I am in New York. Every day—with amazing evenness—she is friendly and smiling, glowing with good nature as she takes me up or down on the elevator.

This is a monotonous job—up and down, up and down, up and down—and I confess that if I were an elevator operator I believe I would be very evil-tempered and spend half the time scheming to change occupations.

But this woman—a pleasant, middle-aged woman—glows with inner self-understanding and projects this to the many people who ride in her elevator. Perhaps she doesn't have much money, but she shares her wealth with others and turns the monotonous up-and-down into an adventure in pleasantness.

The second person is a young fellow whom I don't really know. Someone sent me a clipping from a Toronto, Canada, newspaper with this story about him.

His name is Jim Dillard. He is a football powerhouse in Canada—he was, anyway, until he went into a slump. He just could not get going. He was out of touch with himself; he could not mobilize his feeling about himself as he had been.

Then he read my book *Psycho-Cybernetics*. I understand that members of the champion Green Bay Packers claimed my book helped them, and so did Dillard.

He understood himself once more. He understood that he had to forget the times he'd blundered, and concentrate on his past successes. He understood that he had to carry this confidence of what he had done into the present, making the most of his ability, leaving worry and negative feelings behind.

Jim Dillard regained his old feeling. Once again he was running and blocking crisply, a potent force for his team, the Argos. His understanding of himself as a success was back —and so was his sense of self-respect.

Understanding Yourself

There is one common denominator in these three totally different stories: That understanding must start with yourself.

You live in a complicated, mobile world. The twentieth century has brought with it new freedoms: Of children and adolescents from parents, of women from men, and of minority groups from the Establishment. Our mores are changing; our values may fluctuate.

One thing you must keep constant: Your understanding of yourself.

This is basic.

According to one research project, the difference between "normal" people and mental patients centered around the degree in which they found—or did not find—meaning in their lives. The critical factor, in other words, was that they either understood how to give themselves this meaning, or they did not.

Studies of high school dropouts indicated that 8 to 10 percent had IQs of 110 or over. They dropped out not through lack of intelligence, but through lack of self-understanding and through an inability to realize and cope with their needs.

Other surveys of scholastic underachievers emphasized that they are negative in self-evaluation and at the same time resentful in evaluating others. Again we find the emotional component: The lack of human dignity.

"I work like a slave," you may say, "and I'm always in debt. When I get hold of some money, I'll take time off from my job and then I'll find my self-respect."

Well, maybe you will. I hope so.

Still, leisure time is certainly not the answer for many people. Maybe they start out with great expectations, but studies have pointed to an increase in depression and in suicides on vacations and holidays. Other surveys have shown a correlation between leisure time and juvenile delinquency.

Cicero claimed that "Leisure with dignity is the supremely desirable object of all sane and good men." Although he gave this measured opinion many centuries ago it still stands up today—with one qualification: *if you understand yourself and your needs,* and if your understanding is friendly and supporting.

If not, you will be better off busy, hustling, bustling, but moving toward understanding yourself in a positive way. Busy as you are, you can always find a little time every day to be alone with yourself and to be quiet, to think peacefully, retreating temporarily into a room in your mind to reinvigorate yourself for life's struggles. One thing I understand about myself in my own busy life is that I need a break like this every day. Perhaps you do too.

But more on this later. For now, let us now discuss principles of understanding that will lead you to a greater sense of human dignity.

New Dignity for You

I believe that if you apply my ideas faithfully you will be in a strong position with yourself and with your world, and that you will find a new sense of human dignity is a reality for you.

1. Understand that you are as good as the next fellow. This is extremely important because envy is such a common feeling—perhaps among people of all times, but certainly among people today. The other pastures always look greener; the other fellow has always got it better. You may feel you are always getting a raw deal. Too many people feel that they are inferior. They feel that the other fellow is more worthy—or less guilty—than they are. They feel that he is more mature or more of a he-man, or that he makes more money and that this makes him better. (Or that she is more feminine, giving, or intelligent, and that these qualities make her better.)

You must understand that you are as good as the next fellow. More than this, you must evaluate yourself by your own standards and stop thinking about the next fellow in competitive terms. Do you feel you have to "keep up with the Joneses"? Well, stop it. Let the "Joneses" keep up with you. If you have to compete with somebody, compete with yourself. Every day when you wake up resolve to make this new day a day in which you feel even more strongly the impact of your human dignity. This is a constructive form of competition.

You must determine how good you are. *You* must be the umpire. Forget the next fellow. He's probably moping about what he thinks is *his* inferiority. So help him out. Tell him he's as good as you.

2. Understand the individual nature of your needs. For you *are* an individual; no one else is quite like you. Your needs are individual. You must learn to identify them and, out of your insight, channel your energies toward goals to realize them.

Once again, stop thinking in terms of the needs of other people. Stop bowing to conformist pressures. The needs of this friend or that acquaintance should be irrelevant; you must identify and seek to satisfy *your* needs.

People differ. Some people need to work with their hands; others thrive on mental work. Some come alive when they go to the country or the seashore; others prefer the hustle and bustle of the city. Some people fear and run away from heated arguments; others thrive on them and couldn't live without them.

You must not only *understand* the very individual nature of your needs, you must also *accept* them without self-recrimination if you feel others would feel they make you an inferior sort of person. Remember, you must play the game according to your own rules. Just so long as you don't hurt others in the process, you have a perfect right to call the shots for yourself. Indeed, it is your responsibility to yourself.

As a creature of God, living in His universe, you are an individual and you owe it to yourself to develop in yourself the qualities that arise from your unique needs and to develop to the fullest extent your creative capacities.

3. Understand that you have a right to a life of contentment. This should be self-evident, but it isn't.

So many people feel so negatively about themselves. So many people accuse themselves unceasingly of so many crimes, so many guilts. So many people do not feel they deserve to feel content. They feel guilty about too many things in the past. They keep remembering their past mistakes, their past failures, and when they look at themselves in the mirror they may even hate the sight of themselves.

I know people who always seem to feel guilty. Don't you?

I know people so afraid to express their feelings—including positive feelings like joy and exultation—that they seem to be soldiers on parade, drilling themselves in stoicism and self-denial, anything not to reach a state of pleasure that would threaten them.

During approximately forty years of practice as a plastic surgeon, I have given "new," improved faces to more people than I can remember. It is a thrilling experience each time for me; it is an electrifying experience for the patient—if he can accept the happiness of it all.

Feel it with me. The operation is over. I have long since removed the wrinkles or strengthened the chin or operated on the disfiguring scar. The tissues have been healing; time has worked with me. Now it is time to remove the bandages from the patient's face. I feel humble in my expectation and I remove the bandages; I hand the patient a mirror and await the reaction.

Often this reaction is pure joy. Exultation, excitement, marvel. A "new" face, a new world, a new life. Fantasy may temporarily outdistance reality at this point, granted; but this is legitimately a time of excitement for the individual.

Often, however, the patient is still dissatisfied. The operation has been successful, but he cannot accept his good fortune. He feels he has no right to be happy. His guilt smolders within him. He does not understand that it is his basic right to feel contentment.

You must understand that you were born into this imperfect world to be happy—imperfectly happy, perhaps, but happy. It is your right to achieve this feeling; you must not take it away from yourself. You don't give up your money to anybody who asks for it, do you? Well, then, don't give up your right to contentment.

It doesn't matter if at times you have sinned, erred, blundered; it doesn't matter if you've been inept, weak, stupid; it doesn't matter if you've been clumsy, insensitive, arrogant. All of us at times succumb to our weaknesses; you have, and you will again. The important thing is not to let your guilt and the whole impact of crushing negative feelings take away your knowledge that you have the right to a life of contentment and human dignity.

Understanding Other People

So far in this chapter we have analyzed how to apply understanding to give you a greater sense of human dignity. As we have seen, this understanding must start with understanding of yourself and of your basic needs and rights. It is an understanding you must give yourself. You owe it to yourself. Convicted criminals in our penitentiaries are trying to help themselves through applying my theories of psycho-cybernetics; they have committed anti-social acts and yet they feel they deserve another chance. So why can't you shed your guilt and give yourself a chance to achieve self-respect through understanding?

But once you give yourself this great gift, do not keep it inside and hoard it narcissistically. This would be waste. Exercise your understanding; bring it out into the world of people and share your understanding with others.

Refuse to let narrow-minded hates and prejudices eat into you. Try instead to understand other people—as individuals, not as stereotypes. Other people are unique individuals, too, and you should apply your emotional capacities to relating to them with as much sensitivity and integrity as you have inside you. Once you no longer feel inferior to them, don't turn around and develop another irrational feeling—one of superiority. This too would be self-defeating.

Misunderstanding. There is so much misunderstanding in our struggling, fighting world of people; and understanding among people is so rare by comparison.

Still, if you can give yourself understanding, then you can take one more step and give your understanding to others. As you do, you give yourself the key to your sense of dignity; because the person who can understand and accept both himself and others cannot help but feel his power as a human being with dignity.

You should understand that the other fellow is as good as you—that other people have needs, some quite different from yours. That other people have the right to happiness.

Reach out a helping hand to other people, and think twice before passing judgment on them. You should attune yourself to their aspirations. Nourish yourself as you help them and accept nourishment in return.

As you make a habit of building attitudes of understanding and helpfulness, your respect for yourself grows.

CHAPTER 3

The Active Power of Sincerity

WE are in the process of assembling your power tools for the building of your self-respect: The bulldozers and drills with which you—a construction worker, self-employed—are making yourself a bigger person.

Did you ever watch a building going up, growing day by day through the sweat of many good workingmen? It is no overnight project. Just laying the foundation takes many weeks. If you observe closely, you may see minute progress daily; weekly or monthly observation may show you more surprising developments.

And so it must be with your sense of self-respect. You must work on it, patiently, with dedication, persevering in stormy weather, surviving the winds of bad fortune, refusing to let the inevitable onslaughts of negative feelings pull you under. Sometimes your progress may seem invisible to you—because you are often unobjective and, of course, see yourself every day—but someone who hasn't seen you for months or years may see a striking change.

In building self-respect, we must acquire the ability to develop sound habits that will help us function in a goal-directed, constructive, and humane manner. Such a habit is a wholesome orientation toward life, an orientation of sincerity.

This is not as easy as it seems. Our world is complicated; our mores are changing; our values are confused. In such a climate, millions of people feel cynical. Double-dealing and hypocrisy may seem the only sane way to play the game. Sincerity as a way of life may seem to you foolhardy.

Still, we must more resolutely define our terms. I look on sincerity as an active force, and this concept may be totally new to you. Indeed, in this book I will commend to you other concepts which most people think of as passive—the idea of forgiveness, for example—in an active and dynamic sense.

Sincerity is an active power, if you harness the realistic best in yourself, and project it out into the world where you belong. Sincerity is a dynamic approach to living, if you express your God-given individuality aggressively but constructively.

To know that you do your best to be ethical and honest in your relations with others—in terms of your own willingness to choose this way of conducting yourself—can only improve your feeling of respect for yourself.

What do I mean by sincerity as an active power? I will spell this out for you in this chapter.

First let me say what I do *not* mean. We will not discuss sincerity as a passive concept, in which you exercise naiveté in your dealings with others and turn your other cheek in all innocence to people who might wish to exploit and humiliate you. I see no special virtue in a childish form of sincerity in which you assume that all people are honest and ethical and therefore you might stand helplessly around, a perfect potential victim for any trickster or slickster who might come along scenting an easy mark.

Sincerity, in my meaning—and it is rather a new shade of meaning for me, too—involves an active exercise of constructive power as well as a highly developed sense of sophistication, and it involves also a strong ethical motivation which I feel is at the heart of any individual's genuine self-respect.

The Desire to Do Good

In order to discuss sincerity as an active concept, let us now discuss the ingredients of sincerity.

First, there is the desire to do good. One must feel the desire to make the most of oneself. One must feel strongly the need to be honest with oneself. As an extension of this, one must yearn to give the best of himself to others. When you keep your goodness inside, it stays inside and it does not warm others. It remains a secret to others; and, sooner or later, it may become a secret to yourself, too. Then it is lost, perhaps forever.

Let me read you a letter I received recently. It is a beautiful example of the desire to do good.

> Yesterday the world was ugly and reeked of deception.
>
> At least that is the way it appeared to someone I used to know. A person who had incurred an emotional scar of such proportion that it sank him to the bottommost rung of a ladder suspended in space. All he would have had to do would have been to let go of that last rung and fall to remain forever suspended in the eons of time and fantasy.
>
> But from that pitch blackness of despair came a meager

shaft of light in the form of your superb and startling book titled "Psycho-Cybernetics." Word by word, sentence by sentence and page by page the intensity of the light grew and one by one the rungs of the ladder were ascended. At times most painfully. With each rung the next became easier to reach until firm ground was sighted and the world surrounded and bathed him in the warmth of its brilliant glow of sunshine.

He told me of being reborn in the image of a man, upright, firm in stature, positive in thought and deed and of being ALIVE! Reincarnation in the truest sense of the word. As if by the stroke of a pen the word "impossible" was stricken from his language.

The person I used to know is dead. He is alive. He is I.

Today the world is beautiful.

It was concluded with "I thank you—Your friend for life."

Now I do not write about this letter because my book helped this man—although of course this pleased me more than I can express in mere words—but as an example of what I mean. For this man wanted to do good. Though he had known terrible despair and frustration, his desire to be a sincere, positive person with self-respect remained alive, ready to be ignited—and luckily my book ignited this desire.

In the heat of our competition to outdo each other and to win all our tempting forms of material splendor, we may lose track of this crucial desire to do good and surrender this essential component of sincerity, which in turn is one of the key building blocks of self-respect.

We must win the battle in our minds—our great battle—our battle with negative feelings. The man who wrote me this beautiful letter, expressing his gratitude, knowing it would light up my day for me, he won this battle. It was obviously no easy one for him; he had to pick himself off the floor after he almost went down for the count. Once he regained contact with the positive side of himself, he was not content with this. He wanted me to feel good, too. This is what really impressed me about this letter: his desire to do good.

The great Albert Schweitzer, who wrote about reverence for the life force and about oneness with the many forms of life in the universe, made his words reality with his many deeds of kindness to others. In an active sense, as a healer in a primitive land, he made obvious his desire to do good toward others and in the process lived a life of sincerity and enormous dignity.

This, too, is what I write about.

Keys to Sincerity

You will note, already, that the people I use as examples of sincerity exercise this quality in an active sense.

The man who was helped by my book could have sat in his chair, said "Thank you, very sincerely," and let it go at that. This would be a passive expression of sincerity, but what would it do for him? It was far more feeding for *his* self-respect to come out of his shell and project his good feeling out into the world in an active and potent way, to enrich another human being.

Albert Schweitzer is one of the great geniuses of our time. Schweitzer was a living embodiment of sincerity in action. His desire to do good was no secret. He healed people with his hands, with his books, with his music. He spanned the continents with his active and commandingly potent energy for constructive effort.

Now suppose that we search further for the other keys to an active sincerity that will leave us not passive children to be whipped into submission by the world's bullies, but active builders, potent in the sense of our constructive intentions:

1. Focus on the truth about yourself. It is clear that you cannot be sincere with others until you can focus on the truth about yourself. While this is fundamental, it is doubtlessly the most difficult thing for you to do. You may choose to think charitably about someone else, but you probably expect perfection of yourself. And if you expect yourself to be perfect, you might begin next to hide your faults from yourself so you can find life tolerable.

The trouble is that this sets up a vicious cycle that never ends; insincerity becomes a way of life for you and you forfeit your feeling of self-acceptance.

You must learn to focus on the total truth about yourself —your assets and your liabilities. You must develop the courage to do this. Especially, you must inventory your past successes and your capacity for future successes. The truth need not be negative; truth can be most bolstering.

Focus on the truth about yourself—past, present, and future. Bring back the past now and then to see yourself in proper perspective, but recognize that you cannot live in the past. Look into the future again to see things from a balanced point of view, but understand that you cannot live in the future, either. Then see yourself as you are in the present, and see what you can do to keep focused on this truthful sense of yourself as you are now.

Once again, your chief obstacle to this strengthening, honest type of thinking is your own perfectionism. It is one of the greatest tragedies of our times that so many people expect such impossible things of themselves and cannot allow themselves to see truth because they fear the truth.

The truth about yourself should not disturb you; it should not cause you sleeplessness and self-loathing. You must understand that you have the right to make mistakes sometimes! Everyone does. You have the right to wallow in negation sometimes. Everyone does. And sometimes you have the right to be thoughtless, inconsiderate, fearful, hostile, indecisive, rude, timid. I do not believe that there is an individual in this world who now and then is not a difficult, even impossible person. People are human—not made of marble. Stop feeling you're a criminal when you see yourself in focus. Stop making yourself feel guilty. When you do this, you are a vindictive judge, a vicious jury—you are not giving yourself a fair trial.

In my lectures around the country in recent years, I have stopped off to talk to inmates of more than one penitentiary, including Leavenworth. I have found many of these men— convicted of anti-social offenses—eager for self-improvement, anxious to find the road back to constructive living, quick to ask me questions about my theories of psycho-cybernetics, honest about the negation in much of their lives, searching to remedy it. I was gratified by the response of many prisoners to my lectures, and more than one wrote me following my visit.

My point is this: If these men, who have committed crimes against our very social structure, can forgive themselves, why can't you? What monstrous crime have you committed that you will not allow yourself to take an objective look at yourself without hating yourself?

Focus on the truth about yourself; and then, with full knowledge—the fullest you can give yourself, anyway—accept yourself.

2. Develop an inquiring mind. For proper perspective, you are curious to know the truth about others, too. In a healthy way, you exercise your curiosity. You are interested in them; you try to know them as they are and to appreciate their individuality. You try to learn from their achievements; at the same time, you try to profit from their errors. Through others you strive to improve yourself; if they need you and seek your help, try to help them too. Thus your attempt to know the truth about yourself is an active process. Your mind is attentive and mobile; you adjust yourself to the realities as they appear.

In doing so, you extend your curiosity toward the world you live in—people and all—projecting yourself out toward this world enthusiastically when you wish, or with reserve when you think this approach proper. Your desire for expanding knowledge is alive and active. Your approach is as direct as is practicable. You want to know about life—about yourself, about other people, about your world.

This is not easy. Appearances are often deceiving, and you cannot always be sure your judgment is accurate.

Let me tell you a story; I mentioned it in my book *New Faces: New Futures*, which I wrote over thirty years ago.

Three men who were convinced that they could estimate character on the basis of facial appearance were in my office —a playwright, a lawyer, and a doctor. They studied masks of patients made before surgery.

"This person is a weakling," said the playwright, "this one with the receding chin."

"No," I said. "He is a direct man of business, a stock-broker."

"This fellow with the gash on his cheek," said the lawyer, "he must be a gangster."

"Wrong," I said. "He is a self-effacing businessman who was involved in an auto accident."

It was the doctor's turn. He carefully studied a cast with a broken nose and then gave his opinion: "This man seems to have taken part in a number of fights. He is either a fighter or a racketeer."

"Wrong again," I said. "He fell on his nose when he was a little fellow. He's a schoolteacher."

At this point I showed them the casts made of these patients after surgery, and they expressed their amazement. They found it almost unbelievable that these normal faces had at one time been so disfigured.

Too many of us, however, still hold to the belief that the face is an infallible guide to character and that we—in our great wisdom—can study someone else's face and read his character.

As a plastic surgeon of long experience, I know better—and you should, too. Your quest for knowledge about others and about your world, your development of an inquiring mind, is no overnight matter. You learn actively, interestedly, with a constructive, charged curiosity—but slowly, day by day.

Reject snap judgments. Is a person stupid because he has big ears? Of course not. Is a person swinish because he has a nose with a thick bulbous end? Though even Aristotle believed this was true, it is not so.

Just as you continue to focus on the truth in regard to

yourself, you continue to focus on the truth as it applies to others and to the world you live in.

3. Build your confidence. You cannot reach out to sincerity without confidence. Unless you feel confident, an attitude of sincerity will be merely threatening to you, and not supporting at all.

"I do not feel confident," you say?

Well, then, you must build up your confidence.

How?

By reminding yourself of your past successes, by reliving in your mind your past successes, and by daily keeping your eye on the ball.

I close my eyes and in the room of my mind—in my imagination where I see myself—I am playing golf. I take the proper stance, legs apart, handgrip on the club. Now I prepare to stride into the ball and club it. As I do this, I keep my eye focused on the ball. Wham! I follow through. Most important, I follow through.

This is of course a symbolic exercise, but it is most meaningful. Success will give you confidence.

And what will give you a good chance to nail down successes? Keeping your eye on the ball—your goals—and then following through until you wallop it far and high down the fairway to achieving those goals.

You must remember that life is split-second timing, and you must face the reality of this. We live in a fiercely competitive world; inches may mean the difference between winning and losing, between success and failure. Contrary to popular belief, there may be just a hairline separating the well-paid, confident executive from the scantily paid, low-echelon clerk. Similarly, you may find it hard to discern between the .300 major-league hitter and the fellow who has trouble hitting .230 in the minor leagues.

You build confidence—and therefore a springboard toward an attitude of sincerity—when you keep your eye on the ball and continue to follow through even during days of discouragement. This will win you the successes you need— day after day.

4. See reality. See it as fully as you can, focusing on the truth about yourself, projecting your inquiring mind toward others, building confidence with your active mental approach. Then make your thinking as realistic as you can, refusing to float away into fantasies and refusing to indulge yourself with daydreaming, which may momentarily be pleasant but which will give you no lasting benefits.

One thing should be clear to you: Sincerity will fill you with strength; insincerity will exhaust you. When you deceive yourself and deceive everybody else, you do little or nothing for yourself or others and keeping up the pretense may so tire you out that you have no energy left for real productive activity.

The more sharply you see reality, the less involved you are in fantasy, the more sincere you are capable of being—this is obvious.

What may not be obvious, and perhaps I repeat myself— but this is such an important point—is that seeing reality is no simple process. Reality is not always beautiful—sometimes it is very painful—and you may find it more pleasant temporarily to live in a fool's paradise than in the sometimes bleak world of what is.

Far back in history, men believed in fire and wind gods, and in spirits of the mountains and of the waters. These were aids to them in thinking about the precariousness of their actual existence.

Today, among still-primitive peoples, medicine men still hold sway, reassuring their fellows with their "magic" and sacrificing animals to "appease the gods"—anything to feel a sense of power in coping with the many uncertainties of a dangerous existence.

Well, we may thank our lucky stars that we live a less treacherous existence than this; uncertain as our reality may be, we can usually feel safe in the assurance that the all-powerful natural elements will not bring immediate destruction upon us and that therefore we can face life without the protection of "magic" and "magical thinking."

Even then, facing our realities head-on is not easy. But you must do this to reach your full stature as a human being of dignity.

A Changing You

These are changing times—oh, are they changing times! The world seems to change a little almost every day; we try to keep pace with the changes.

But the most important changes are usually internal; and a positive change for you is one in which you adjust your attitudes—toward yourself, toward others—in the direction of greater sincerity.

If insincerity and pretense and endless affectation have been your habitual pattern, you may not find change effortless.

Adjusting to newness is rarely effortless. Children have been shown to be disturbed on listening to altered nursery rhymes. Dogs have barked and whined at the unfamiliar sight of their masters walking on their hands. Any newness—any change in habitual pattern—may cause anyone emotional upset. The adult who overeats or smokes or drinks too much may find the adjustment to moderation positively unsettling.

Still, our objective is a changing you. To move toward your full self-respect as a human being, you must move toward the greatest degree of sincerity that you can attain, however difficult that may be at first.

To review my main points, this is an active form of sincerity, in which you go beyond lip service, helplessness or wishful resignation—to a kinetic, functional, and dedicated participation in your own improvement as a person who lives in a particular local community which is part of a larger community which is part of a world community.

The passively sincere person may be in favor of improved education for disadvantaged children and let it go at that. Time for a nap.

The actively sincere person will—if he possibly can—do something about it. If he is a school administrator or teacher, he will practice what he preaches. If he is not, he may make an active attempt to implement his ideas as a PTA member or community helper, or perhaps as a donor of money, or he might help to campaign for political office-seekers who agree with his ideas.

The passively sincere person may believe in more ethical business dealings—in principle.

The actively sincere person will put it on the line. In his business dealings he will be as ethical and honest as he can possibly be without jeopardizing his position vis-à-vis his competitors. True, he will not always be able to reach his ideals in actual conduct; sometimes this would amount to cutting his own throat—which he would not do, and I certainly would never suggest that he should.

As I mentioned earlier, I am not suggesting that you turn the other cheek and let people without ethical scruples push you around. I am also not suggesting that you assume that just because you are moving toward sincere attitudes and sincere actions, others will reciprocate. I am also not trying to make you believe that this is a world of inexhaustible goodness, a world in which you can blindly put your faith in others who have not proved that they merit your faith.

My concept of sincerity—and you may find it a rather new concept—is one in which you try to be honest with yourself and with others and to play a worthwhile constructive role in your world *when this is possible.*

It goes without saying that sincerity is not always possible, that it would be foolish to try to be sincere with some people. Adolf Hitler, for example, was such a man. Perhaps Neville Chamberlain thought his best path was to be candid with Hitler. I don't know what he was thinking, of course— but, if so, he was unwise. Hitler is the perfect prototype of the person you should not try to be sincere with.

Still, with yourself, and with many people, you may work toward sincerity—as an active power giving meaning to your life and substance to your budding skyscraper of self-respect.

There are doctors who, above and beyond financial reward, want to help people feel healthier. There are lawyers who, of course, want to get their fees paid, but also want to help their client. We have entertainers who want to give people enjoyment and judges who want to render just decisions and waiters who want to make your meal pleasant and typists who try to make letters look attractive. These people are living examples of my conception of sincerity as an active, dynamic life force.

Carlyle believed that society was based on hero worship. I

think he was right—and I think it is too bad he was right, because you must be your own hero.

What good does it do you to look at someone else—a "hero"—and tell yourself that he is wonderful? You must tell yourself that *you* are wonderful. You must give yourself credit for what you are as a human being. You must build in yourself a sense of self-respect that can make you feel wealthier than any millionaire. Start by building with understanding; then move the emphasis to sincerity. Start today, start now.

I have a friend who has a little girl who resists going to sleep. When bedtime comes, she seems to sense it and is ready to fight. She will go to bed on time, she says, "Monday, Tuesday, Wednesday." Her parents are indulgent, and therefore the result is predictable: She never goes to bed on time.

Don't you put off your building of self-respect until "Monday, Tuesday, Wednesday." That really means "Mañana," "mañana" means "tomorrow," and chances are that "tomorrow" means "never." So, start today.

Are you building your bank account? Fine. Are you building your professional status? Wonderful. Are you building a family? More power to you. Whatever you are building for yourself and for others in your world is fundamental to your life.

As you build, as you set your goals and move toward them, make self-respect the cement that binds them and that gives them meaning. Give your activities meaning and power as you intermesh them with understanding and sincerity.

CHAPTER 4

Winning Out Over Uncertainty

OUR approach to self-respect will be an active and functional one. We aim at a sense of human dignity that is real; we descend from our ivory towers and plant our feet in the solid soil of our common humanity. What we want is more than an abstract concept, more than a fleeting thought—useful as these may be to us. We will transcend passivity and, hopefully, go on to the implementation, not only of ideas and images that will help us respect ourselves, but also of real goals that will improve our station in life and bring us inner satisfaction as well.

First, in other words, we build our good feeling about ourselves. Second, we do something about this good feeling. We use it. We extend it out into the world of people and feel the power of exercising it constructively.

In this book, we will do more than verbalize abstraction. Later on, we will get very practical and tackle some exercises together, exercises for the stimulation of your emotional muscles. Goal-builders, I will call them. We will see what goal-building we can do together in furthering our common search for a self-respect that has its roots both in inner acceptance and in an adaptation to reality.

We will focus on the positive. We will be Walt Whitmans all, as we "sing" of the positive and try to channel our energies into our drive for the positive.

But we are forgetting something—my long experience tells me this. You were not born yesterday? Shake hands on that, friend; neither was I. What about our negative feelings? What about our fears of disaster? What about our impossible mornings? What about those days when even a quick glance in the mirror is traumatic?

I feel strongly that to build the positive and ignore the negative is building on quicksand. Although we must continue our positive approach, of course, we must also prepare ourselves to deal with the negative feelings that threaten to destroy us.

And first of all, we must learn to cope with uncertainty. We must not let life's uncertainties frighten us into a retreat from life. We must refuse to let them make us immobile and dissociated, to play everything safe, and to take no chances, straddling the fence at all times.

We must win out over uncertainty; we must lose our fear of uncertainty; and we must live with uncertainty.

We must look upon life's many uncertainties with adult eyes. They will not vanish if we wave our "magic wand" and say "go away"—that is, if you will permit me a very small joke, no self-respecting uncertainties will do this.

Uncertainty has always been with us. When the world was born, uncertainty was born. Birth and death—we have always known these uncertainties. Weather—we have always lived with the sudden onslaughts of lightning and blinding rains from the skies, of violent typhoons sweeping over our seas, and of ferocious hurricanes swirling over our land, destroying with a frightening and impersonal fury.

Down through history, people have felt an insecurity about each other, and this almost-inevitable insecurity has led to the possibly endless series of wars which have spread-eagled the pages of our history books. In a sense, one could characterize the story of civilization as a story of wars—national wars, religious wars, civil wars—and in recent years, as transportation's and communication's progress makes the world grow smaller, we have world wars. Human civilization has not been able to escape from wars and the scars that come from wars, these destructive manifestations of uncertainty.

Today uncertainty is still with us—in all these ways, and more. We are uncertain of our civilized rules, which are all changing constantly. We are uncertain about our objectives; we do not seem to know where we are going. Further, we are uncertain of our status; we live in a highly mobile and competitive world and in our struggles to keep up with others we may lose touch with ourselves.

So, in summary, to build self-respect, we must learn to live with the potential negation of uncertainty; and that's what we will discuss in the pages of this chapter.

Living Hopefully with Anxiety

And so, how do you win out over uncertainty?

First, I feel strongly that you must learn to live with the fear that uncertainty brings, on positive and hopeful terms. If you can handle this fear, this anxiety, if you do not allow it to dominate you, then you are on the right track.

This is not always easy to do, it goes without saying. In my travels around the country, hundreds—no, thousands—of people have talked to me about how their uncertainties have obsessed them, making their lives little but painful question marks: Will the boss fire them? Will their spouse leave them? Will the dreaded nuclear holocaust come to reality? Will they lose their money? Will a loved one in the hospital die?

What can I tell them? How can I help them? With no miracles, surely. Just with common sense and with insight. I tell them that their problems are not theirs alone—they are universal. Everywhere we find problems and uncertainties. The person with self-respect wrestles with them; the person who lacks self-respect drowns.

Let me tell you about a tragedy from my own life; it might help you with the tragedies in your life, so that you can adjust to them.

A birthday party for my mother was in progress. I gave it for her and many, many people came to my apartment on top of a medical building in central Manhattan. Actors, doctors, lawyers, businessmen, wives, career women filled the apartment and overflowed onto the terrace. Music, dancing, drinking, eating, laughter, spirited conversation. An orchestra serenaded us. Life seemed joyful. It was a happy occasion for me—at first.

My mother's old friends were there, too, her old friends from many years gone by; one, very gay, was singing her old favorite songs.

I had a splendid evening. I talked to my friends, I reminisced with my mother's old friends, I enjoyed what I thought was my mother's pleasure in the occasion. In a way,

I felt detached; I mostly savored the feeling that I had done something to make my mother happy. Too many of my mother's birthdays had come and gone unnoticed; not this one.

But at three in the morning, when the guests were gone, my mother and I stood alone on the terrace. She told me then that she had cancer of the breast. My satisfaction, of course, vanished, and in a second I felt only fear and despair and sorrow. Her death, about a year later, was one of the big tragedies of my life.

It was not easy for me to recover. For a while I sat around and moped; I could not accept such a terrible thing happening. I cried for my mother—and for my loss. But what could I do? I could not forever bemoan life's sorrows, life's dangers, life's uncertainties.

One day I remembered an old Irish proverb one of my mother's friends had told me many years before, when I was a small boy: "If God shuts one door, He opens another."

I couldn't complain to God, I realized. I must fight my way back to my feet and feel again the way I had when I was planning my mother's birthday party. Even though it was in a sad way, I *had* given her pleasure with her birthday party—her huge birthday party—before she died. I realized that I had to place my hand, once again, on the knob of the door, ready to open it and walk into the opportunities of today and tomorrow, leaving the disappointments of the past behind me and not fearing the uncertainties ahead.

That's what I did, and that is also what you must do. You must learn to live with the anxieties and the depression that life's uncertainties bring—and you must live hopefully, too.

You, too, know your disappointments, your tragedies, your heartaches and your frustrations—and you must learn to rise above negation to surmount them and live as best as you can, with your sense of self-respect still alive in the midst of imperfection.

Many social critics have called this an "age of anxiety." Maybe so. But it can also be an age in which, in spite of your anxieties, you live most productively.

Close your eyes now and, in your imagination, see this picture: A doctor is checking a patient's blood pressure. He finds that a condition of high blood pressure exists. As tactfully as he can, but honestly too, he tells the patient this, and he advises him on relaxing and getting adequate rest, and perhaps he prescribes some medication, too.

Now, if you have high-blood-pressure-type reactions to the anxieties that uncertainty brings, you must "prescribe" for yourself.

For one thing, you must understand that your frequent frustrations and small crises are not unique. Life is no bed of roses for anyone, and people who think it is must adjust such unrealistic preconceptions. Anticipate the uneven flow of life so that the shocks do not unseat you.

In his book, *Don Budge: A Tennis Memoir* (Viking Press, 1969), the tennis great tells a classic story of successful adaptation to an anxious, uncertain situation.

It was 1936, and Budge was locked up with Fred Perry in a tense semifinal match at Wimbledon as 18,000 people watched from the stands. They had split the first two sets, and every point was crucial. Then, during a volley, a little piece of newspaper drifted down from the stands—and Perry, about to make an easy shot, paused, neglected to hit the ball, and instead watched the paper as it sailed to the ground.

An outstanding tennis player, Fred Perry also had great presence on court. While 18,000 watched, stunned, he calmly walked over, picked the paper off the ground, and began to read it. Then he started to laugh. He laughed and laughed and laughed. He laughed so hard he had to hold his stomach.

His laughter was infectious. Soon the crowd, bewildered as they were, joined him in his laughter.

At the other side of the court, Budge waited, his curiosity growing. Finally Perry beckoned him, and he ran to the net to see what was so funny.

It was nothing at all. Something very mundane—maybe a weather report—was on the piece of newspaper, but, out of the side of his mouth, Perry told Budge to laugh.

And laugh Budge did. He laughed, Perry laughed, and everybody who had come to see the semifinal match at Wimbledon laughed and laughed.

Suddenly Perry decided it had served its purpose. He stuck the paper in his pocket and went back to play tennis once more. Things quieted down again, the sedate tennis atmosphere returned, and Perry and Budge slashed at the ball once more—with the same old efficient fury. But, doubtless, they were more relaxed and more competent than before, if that was possible.

A semifinal match at historic Wimbledon. What a creative, masterly, daring way to eat into the pressure! What a superb reaction to anxiety and uncertainty! What a lesson for living in our "age of anxiety"!

Of course, there are some things you can't laugh at. There is nothing funny about poverty, disease, war, death, deprivation.

But for the ordinary uncertain, anxiety-producing crisis situation, tennis player Perry's tactics are superb. While you're here, while you have the great gift of life, laugh whenever you can; and, extracting the real meaning from this story, those times can be frequent if we aim at creating the laughter.

Don't Take Uncertainties Personally

I have, especially in the last three or four years, talked to many people around the country and am coming to realize that many people who feel most hopeless about their anxieties and their uncertainties seem to believe that their problems are unique.

This, of course, is not so. Everyone is at sea these days, and everyone feels at times that he is drowning. So don't take your uncertainties so personally, and then maybe you will be able to navigate your fragile craft through the stormy waves to the safety of the shore.

Everyone must cope with problems and uncertainties and anxieties; everyone makes mistakes—even dangerous mistakes. Everyone in living exposes himself to the dangers others may bring him and exposes others to the dangers he may bring them.

One evening I wanted to get to a hospital quickly. But it was six o'clock, and New York's streets were jammed with traffic, as usual. I jumped into a taxi at Fifty-seventh Street, asking the driver to enter Central Park at Sixth Avenue and go through to the West 106th Street exit. I thought that this route would help us bypass the heavy traffic.

The cabdriver didn't listen too well. He drove to Seventy-second Street, swerved left, and headed westward. Near the West Seventy-second Street exit, I reminded him that I had asked him to take a different route.

"Oh," he said, "I forgot." I could see he was not acting; he was truly annoyed with himself.

"Anyone can make a mistake," I said. "Forget it."

"I hate to make mistakes like that," he said. "I don't know what's the matter with me." He cursed himself out with a few unprintable remarks.

"It can happen," I said. "We'll get there just about as fast, anyway. Don't worry about it!"

"Yeah, but I don't like myself when I make mistakes like that." He continued to berate himself while we waited at the Seventy-second Street exit for the traffic light to change.

"It's all right," I said.

"I shouldn't do that," he said.

Finally, he got me where I wanted to go, but he was still angry with himself. On the way we witnessed a near-disaster. A car made a left turn as a pedestrian crossed the street. The pedestrian, who had the right of way, kept walking, raising his hand imperiously toward the superior strength of the vehicle, which kept moving. It was a close call. Two more mistakes: A careless driver and a stubborn, in-the-right pedestrian.

On this one short cab ride to a hospital there were three mistakes in all—and the two-sided mistake was almost a disaster. This is the human condition, so face it resolutely.

Of the three persons who made mistakes, my driver's mistake was by far the most harmless. All he did was delay me a few minutes. Yet he was doing such damage to himself! He lashed into himself as critically as if his small mistake was tragic and unique.

But we must realize that mistakes are part of us—mistakes and problems and uncertainties and anxieties and frustrations—like bacteria in the throat or tension in our urban, fast-moving environment. We need all these imperfections, in a sense, so that we can master them and develop in ourselves a tough and resilient strength in order to live imprecisely yet resourcefully in our scrambling world.

Remember this:

If your boss fires you, you are not the only one who ever lost a job. Stop hating him or blaming yourself. Be practical about it; rest up and when you're ready, go look for another spot.

A friend may reject you—a good friend, an old friend; shocking as this may be, you are not the only one to whom this has happened. Hating him will do you no good—it will harm you. You can do without such a friend. Your best friend is yourself, anyway; and you can make another friend later on when you meet someone you like.

If you get sick—you are not the only one.

If you lose your money—you are not the only one.

With very few exceptions, no matter what happens to you, you are not the only one.

It is important for you to remember this, so that you don't take uncertainties, heartaches, and problems too personally. Then you can concentrate on the main point—accepting yourself and respecting yourself as you wrestle with your crises, and seeking practical answers that will help you to improve your status in the world and give richer meaning to your existence.

A Winning Approach to Uncertainty

And so we all live in uncertainty. We must build self-respect in spite of uncertainty.

We are not omnipotent, and we must admit this to ourselves. Hard as we may try to exercise a constructive control over our destinies, we can never be successful all the time. I have my tragedies and my defeats and my depressions to endure; you have yours.

The question is: How do you rise above uncertainty? How do you develop a winning approach to uncertainty?

1. Renounce passivity as a way of life. You refuse to give in to helplessness. You don't just sit back and let things happen. You do not see yourself as a victim of life's vicissitudes —even when things go wrong. You do not retreat from life in a panic during stormy weather.

2. Renounce neutrality as a way of life. Perhaps neutrality works all right for nations (Switzerland survived two world wars thus), but the neutral person does not live fully. When life's uncertainties and insecurities frighten you into repeated assumptions of neutral attitudes, you give up part of yourself in the process. There may be times, of course, when it would be prudent to straddle the fence, to remain silent, or to express no opinion. To insure your survival, sometimes your best approach may be one of absolute neutrality; I would never recommend that you ever expose yourself or loved ones to any danger through reckless or needless actions or statements.

Nevertheless, though you may at times find it expedient or wise to assume neutral attitudes, you must still renounce neutrality as a way of life. Whenever you can, get off the fence. Whenever you can, shrug off life's insecurities and take a stand. Whenever you can, you take pride in the expression of your individuality. Whenever you can, you come out of hiding—knowing that you are a person of genuine worth.

3. Choose an active approach to life. Instead of letting life's insecurities floor you, hang in there and counterpunch, like a courageous boxer. Stop thinking about what life can do to you and start thinking about what you can do for yourself.

In this book I stress an active approach because I am coming to understand more and more that ideas and images—though crucially fundamental in importance—are not in themselves always enough. Thus I have written of sincerity as an active concept, and in a later chapter I will discuss my conception of active forgiveness.

It is the passive person who is always obsessed with what the world will do to him; the active person may be too busy *doing* to worry.

Though Babe Ruth may have struck out many times, I doubt if he worried about it much when he stood at home plate, bat in hand; he was too busy thinking about hitting a home run.

Similarly, every time Joe Louis stepped into a ring, he could have mulled over the possibility that he'd get hurt; he probably didn't, however—he was too busy planning a quick knockout of the other man.

The active approach is the approach with which one has a fighting chance to win out over life's multiple dangers.

4. Set goals. Every day set goals, then move out to achieve them. The nature of the goal is not important; what is important is what you feel for it. If you feel real enthusiasm for your goals, you will keep thinking about the steps you will take to reach them; you will not waste your time worrying about every adverse possibility.

In my theory of psycho-cybernetics I stress the basic importance of goals for the individual who wants to get the most out of his life. Later we will consider goals in greater detail in terms of your achieving maximum human dignity.

5. Allow yourself mistakes. Allow them just because you aim to be reasonable with yourself, and it is reasonable that you will make plenty of mistakes during your lifetime. It is obvious to anyone who thinks objectively about it that the only person who can avoid making mistakes is the person who never tries to do anything.

This is a key idea—life is uncertain enough, and if you compound its uncertainties by criticizing yourself for your mistakes, you are likely to remain passive through fear and buckle under to life's forces.

Here's a thought that may help you: You win out over life's uncertainties, as a rule, only when you are able to accept your own uncertainties.

The Secure Person in an Anxious Age

I think it is possible for a mature, thinking, productive person to feel secure—even in an anxious age such as ours.

Anyway, is this such an anxious age? Is this century more difficult than past centuries? Today, it is true, we live knowing that devastating weapons exist which could blow up the world. It is also true that this century has witnessed the most horrifying tragedy in human history—the massacre of six million Jewish people in Hitler's Nazi Germany.

Basic personality change through "brainwashing" is, on a lesser scale, another frightening development in our hectic times.

But other ages have known other inhumanities and other terrors.

In the eleventh, twelfth, and thirteenth centuries, the Crusades to the Holy Land brought brutal savagery and destruction to people in the name of religion.

From Genghis Khan to Napoleon, power-mad despots have over and over again bloodied the face of the world.

Human history has endured many barbarous customs: Legal authorities, many centuries ago, had the power to remove a man's tongue if he was an alleged blasphemer; insane people many decades ago were kept in chains; witches—in reality just simple women—were burned to death. Kings held absurd and total power over people, and the insidious practice of slavery cheated millions of their right to freedom.

All this is very morbid—I write of it only because I hear, in my travels, so much about how impossible it is to live sensibly these days, whereas to the best of my knowledge insecurity and injustice have always been part of the human condition.

I am merely trying to indicate the insecure nature of our world and the necessity of your overcoming these negative possibilities to move toward your attainment of our common goal—self-respect.

Once again, I reaffirm my belief that it is possible for a mature and sensibly directed person to feel both security and self-respect in this age of anxiety, as it has been possible in all the ages of anxiety throughout history.

In sum, to do this you must: Learn to live with anxiety; understand the universal, not personal, nature of uncertainty and of ill fortune; and adopt a dynamic approach to life so that you can outlast bad times and go on to good times.

In the process, you must accept yourself when external events let you down or when you let yourself down. You must not be like the cab driver I wrote about who was so intolerant of his minor mistake.

There have been recently quite a few carefully designed programs to help backward children achieve reading skills. One of the fundamental aims was to change the emotional orientation of these children—diverting them from the stumbling block of their anxiety and sense of inadequacy, and motivating them toward goal attainment.

Most of you have no trouble reading, but you may have plenty of trouble dealing with life's uncertainties. I hope that this chapter helps you to free yourself from anxiety and, as in the case of these backward children, moves you toward a sense of goal attainment.

If you are a housewife, keeping a home that is safe, clean, and attractive is commendable, and your family will appreciate it. Something is wrong, however, if you spend all your spare time worrying about it.

If you are a salesman, it is reassuring that you have just made some strong sales. There is something off-center if you find yourself tortured about your next sale.

If you are a college student, it is promising that you have earned good grades in all your courses. Why then are you fretting about your senior year?

If you are a business executive, your raise in pay is good news—your wife will be happy. Why do you keep getting upset every time you speak to your boss for more than five minutes?

If you are a pretty young girl turned twenty-one, marriage may be a satisfying goal for you. Why are you fearful about whether you will ever get married?

Uncertainties here? Yes, legitimate uncertainties. The question is: Can you win out over your many uncertainties—or do they win out over you?

When your uncertainties are winning out over you, re-reading this chapter should help you to turn the tables.

This is very important for you. If you can win out over your uncertainties and over your other negative feelings, you are well on the way to consolidating your feeling of inner strength and of respect for yourself.

CHAPTER 5

Your Struggle
to Overcome Resentment

WHEN I write, I do more than pound a typewriter or fill up pages of paper. I try to visualize the people who will read the book. Who are they? What are they like? What do they want from me? How can I help? I ask myself these questions.

In a very real sense, I have a head start here because, lecturing in almost every state of the nation during the last ten years, I have seen your faces and I have talked to you and I know more than a little about your problems and responsibilities and worries.

I have seen in my audiences businessmen, absorbed in the competitive money-fight, scrambling to make enough money to rear their children, involved in tensions at work and at home—in many cases.

I have seen housewives, wrestling with their own special pressures, unsung heroines of the home, trying to adapt their thinking to changing ways, trying to figure out sound ways to bring up their children.

I have seen youth—high school and college—earnestly seeking to formulate values, looking for the road to good living, trying to get off on the right foot.

And I have seen Senior Citizens—often (too often) retired from Life's battles, sometimes still in it—seeking answers for their own special problems.

I have lectured to many, many thousands of people—so different, and yet so similar—about making something of their lives, about finding themselves, about achieving for themselves a sense of their unique human dignity.

Self-respect; that's what it's all about.

But, as I've said, in seeking self-respect, you must do more than sharpen your positive forces; you must also develop the capacity to overcome your negative, destructive tendencies.

Such as uncertainty, which we discussed at some length in the last chapter; and such as resentment, which we will now consider.

Resentment is a fundamental component of the failure mechanism, which I have written about often in detailing my theory of psycho-cybernetics. It is a dread enemy, because at one time or another everybody feels it. It is a universal phenomenon, unfortunately.

I close my eyes and see again in my imagination the tens of thousands of people who have come to my lectures—so many different types of people, but all sometimes must wrestle with their resentment.

I close my eyes and imagine you, the many people who will read this book—so many different types of people, but you, too, will all at times find you must try to smother the fires of your resentment.

And I, too—again and again—must marshal my constructive forces and put to rout my own resentment. The terrible thing about resentment is that it may become a marathon—unending, chronic, spreading.

Indeed, resentment spreads like an infectious disease. When we feel strong resentment, we spread it to others because others react to our resentment with more resentment. Moreover, feeling annoyed with us for initiating the feeling and irritated with themselves for latching on, they may then drench themselves in resentment and unleash it on others who, by bad fortune, find themselves in their path. This is the negative contribution that a resentful person has to make to other people.

Suppose that you are eating foods which are causing you to become overweight. You become sluggish, and you find that you are beginning to worry about your health. What do you do? Well, if you are making a genuine effort to be constructive, perhaps you change your diet.

Now resentment is one of the foods in our emotional diet. It is an unpalatable goulash of negativism and unrelieved frustration. It is an unappetizing stew seasoned with bad temper, envy, and revenge—a horrible concoction worthy of the witches from *Macbeth*, but not worthy of you.

The result? Emotional indigestion, a mental ulcer moving toward becoming a very real physical ulcer.

What to do? Again, change your diet. You need more nutrition, with less waste and over-sharp seasoning.

You must eliminate the resentment from your emotional diet. It won't be easy; the feeling of resentment warms like fire and has the fascination of fire. You must struggle to overcome this negative and destructive inner fire; you must struggle to pour water on its crackling flames. You are your own fireman; you brave flames and smoke and heights to win over fire and save a life—your life.

Yes, it is your life you save when you extinguish the spreading flames of resentment. For, with resentment, you may or may not hurt others, but there is one person you are certain to destroy—yourself.

In fighting resentment, we fight to save our most human and most precious feeling—our feeling of self-respect.

The Resentment Complex

We all know about the inferiority complex. We have read about it so much that we may cringe at the impact of the mere phrasing.

But what about the Resentment Complex—that ghastly marathon, that dance around destruction, that cycle of endless negation?

Here are its components, briefly spelled out for you to escape, not to emulate. In dodging them and embracing positive qualities, you enrich yourself. Afterward, I will spell it out in greater detail.

1. *Revenge.*
2. *Envy.*
3. *Sulkiness.*
4. *Elimination from life.*
5. *Narrow-mindedness.*
6. *Temper.*
7. *Mistake-mindedness.*
8. *Enmity.*
9. *Negligence.*
10. *Tension as a habit.*

1. Revenge. You feel you have been wronged. You are a victim of injustice, you tell yourself. So you plan your revenge—not just for a few minutes, or a few hours, but every day, as a way of life.

Maybe you have been wronged. But, why dwell on it for a lifetime? Whom do you destroy with your fantasies of revenge? The person you hate? No, you destroy yourself. The fires of revenge consume you. You do not sleep well. You do not work well. You do not eat well. Your obsession with revenge spins you round and round, trapped in your Resentment Complex.

2. Envy. Another feeling you can do without. When you envy someone else, you depreciate yourself and you resent the other person. Again, you trap yourself in an endless cycle of negation.

Stop envying! Instead, work to build your self-image. If you feel good about yourself, you will not waste your time feeling envy.

3. Sulkiness. The honeymoon is over, and you find yourself in an unglamorous world, living your usual unglamorous life, making compromises, and moving from problem to problem.

Your bright moment—whatever it was—is over, temporarily at least. Your reality is not constantly exhilarating. How do you react to this? With sulkiness? Pouting, sluggish sulkiness? If so, you head straight for negation, for a cycle of negation I call your Resentment Complex.

The alternative? Set new goals for your imperfect self in our imperfect world and move toward creative living.

4. Elimination from life. You fear competition. "Suppose I lose," you tell yourself. And so, taking no chances, you eliminate yourself from life.

But, when you do this, you also eliminate yourself from joy and usefulness and eventually you become useless to yourself as well. Frustrated in your web of fear and withdrawal, you quickly fall prey to resentment—and living with a Resentment Complex is no joyride.

5. *Narrow-mindedness.* You restrict your outlook. You tighten your feelings. You put tight shoes on your feet, handcuffs on your wrists, and pull up on your necktie until you fear you won't be able to breathe.

Then what?

Resentment comes. It flows through you like spreading fire, in reaction to imprisonment. Your narrow-mindedness plunges you into resentment, and until you learn to look at life with a gentle perspective and kind eyes, you will live in the dark world of resentment.

6. *Temper.* Temper is the explosive end product of the Resentment Complex. Envy, disappointment and frustration build up in our lives, until smouldering resentment finally bursts into the flames of temper.

7. *Mistake-mindedness.* When you live with resentment, you live with mistaken-mindedness. We are all mistake-prone, but there are questions of degree. We will make mistakes as long as we live, but the mistake of resentment is especially regrettable because it is self-destructive and leads us into pockets of tension from which we find it very hard to escape.

8. *Enmity.* The sharpest and deadliest claw of resentment. It can be even more destructive than revenge, because your revenge obsession may focus on one or two people, while your feeling of enmity is a disease which you wish to unleash upon all people.

Enmity as a way of life is cancerous. You must destroy it, or it will destroy you.

9. Negligence. When you wake up in the morning, do you scramble out of bed and, without hesitation, rush out your front door and head for your place of employment?

Of course not. If you did, you would be guilty of negligence toward yourself since other people at your office or factory would see you, disheveled and in your nightclothes and—well, let's not carry this fantasy any further, because I can't bear to describe your boss's reaction.

Thus, on arising mornings, you dress, brush your teeth, shave or apply lipstick, and so on. You do not neglect your appearance.

This is one form of negligence; another is emotional negligence.

The emotionally negligent person wallows in resentment. Instead of steering himself toward constructive goals, he lives aimlessly, drifting in frustration, developing a Resentment Complex.

10. Tension. When resentment becomes a habit, so does tension. For resentment and tension are twins—not identical, but twins nonetheless. Everyplace one goes, you will find the other. They are not pleasant either: you would be better off not knowing them.

The Resentment Complex is a composite of negative forces; of revenge and envy, negligence and narrow-mindedness—the culmination of which is tension.

This negative, destructive buildup of poisonous, unreleasable feeling leads inevitably to resentment and tension.

Resentment Complex: DANGEROUS, KEEP AWAY.

How do you avoid this complex? In a way, that is the subject of this book. For resentment and self-respect do not mix well. And, in the process of building your sense of self-respect, and reaching out with it to other people, chances are that you will deliver a knockout blow to your resentment.

The Destructiveness of Misguided Resentment

Earlier, I described the wild gang fights of my boyhood. Bricks, bats, sticks, stones, kettles, and shields—two gangs of boys unleashing resentment upon each other.

These were warm-weather battles, most of the time. As in today's riots, warm weather seemed a factor in firing up physical outbursts of violence. But we smoldered in the winter, too. It would snow, and we would build huge mounds of snow on streetcorners and the violence would take on a different—and generally milder—pattern. Throwing snowballs at each other was harmless fun, but iceballs were products of nastiness.

I remember one fight vividly: This kid stood on top of the pile of snow, crowing that he was the leader, when another kid came up and at short range hurled an iceball at his head, knocking him down. Slumped in the snow, unconscious for a while, the leader did not move and everyone was scared: blood trickled from a horrible gash on his forehead, flowing over his right eye, then onto the snow, dyeing it red-brown. Luckily he recovered consciousness in the hospital and was stitched up—one victim of resentment who recovered.

"Well," you can say, "boys will be boys."

But if you say this, you don't get the distinction. Growing boys need outlets for their aggression—this goes without saying—and such outlets as competitive athletics (or snowball fights) are helpful in this sense.

But iceballs are not snowballs, and the kid who threw the iceball aimed at the leader's head was expressing destructive resentment. He was, incidentally, from the leader's own gang and perhaps was trying to hurt him out of envy of his status.

Surprisingly, the victim, once recovered, gloried in his wound, feeling that the scar on his forehead was some kind of medal for bravery. In summertime, when we swam in the East River, he would repeatedly call attention to the scar on his forehead.

What a mistaken concept of bravery! How much braver the policeman who, that same winter, saw a kid struggling in the ice-cold waters of the East River and who, with his overcoat on, plunged into the waters to save him!

The Torture of Resentment in Fantasy

Now these gang fights of ours, resentment exploding into action, they were externally destructive.

Resentment does not always take this path. Sometimes it stays inside and smolders and the poor suffering resentful person must endure the torture of his unhappy fantasies and obsessions, poisoning himself with his thoughts, destroying his self-respect, reducing his positive instincts to ashes with the fire that burns inside him.

Recently, two unhappy men came to see me to talk over their problems and to see if they could help themselves in the process. Both struggled under the burden of their resentment. Both buried their creative, positive energies under the fury of their hate. Both could not find the sense of human dignity to which they were entitled.

Coincidentally, both tortured themselves with repeated,

intense fears that followed an identical yet opposite pattern. They both feared choking to death—one, that he would choke somebody; the other, that someone would choke him. Resentment smoldering within—a terrible force.

In telling you their stories I will of course not reveal their names or identify them in any way. I tell you their stories—in this anonymous way—so that you, reading my book, can benefit from their experience without injuring them in any way.

One man was a middle-aged salesman. He was living in the past. He had grown up with a sense of inferiority, and he projected this feeling toward me.

His mother, he told me, talking to me in my living room, was an old woman now. But still he hated and feared her.

He feared being close to her. He feared that if he were close to her, living with her, visiting her, she would choke him. He feared that she would kill him.

Obviously, this was extremely unrealistic. To find out how he came to think this way, I asked him about his background.

It was an unfortunate one—he had come from a broken home. He was only a few years old when his father deserted his mother. He had been an only child, and his mother gave up her life to tend for him. She left a good job to take a less lucrative one so that she could take better care of him. She gave him all her attention, fussed over him, centered her life around him.

This, of course, was terrible. A boy needs to get out into the world, to explore it, and to feel confidence as he experiences a growing ability to deal with that very real world. He was deprived of all this. His mother, deserted, needed him—or, at least, she felt she did. So she smothered him. Deep into his adolescent years, they spent much time together. In fact, they were inseparable. He needed to feel separate and on his own, with an identity that was his.

This was the unfortunate background of this middle-aged salesman who came to see me in his unhappiness, struggling to find fulfillment in an uncertain and competitive world, struggling to overcome the burden of a past which had been none of his doing.

His life was not all negative. He was a fairly adequate salesman; he had some satisfactions now and then. But, still, he drifted from job to job, was frightened by a self-destructive urge in himself and, unmarried, he had few good friends. He drank too much, felt guilty, and was worried by the perverse pleasure he felt in doing the wrong thing. Sometimes, he told me, he seemed—against his conscious will—to be trying to lose his job.

Most pronounced, though, was his strong feeling of resentment toward his mother. He hadn't lived in the same home with her for many years, in a physical sense, but his mind was full of her, of his hate for her, of his endless resentment of her.

He was free of her, but he was not free of her—the resentment burned on, an endless marathon dancing around in his imagination day and night.

Another man came to see me recently—a good-looking man, married, with one child, who told me how one night he woke up and, horrified, found that he was beginning to choke his wife.

Another story of a burning, long-smoldering resentment —not really toward his wife. It was toward his father that he felt this.

Still, his wife became the unwitting object of his almost-acted-out resentment. She considered it a bad dream the first time it happened, but it happened again. Several other times, it did not reach such an extreme state, but nevertheless he felt the urge to choke her.

Anxious and horrified with himself, this man sat across from me and told me of all this. He loathed himself for this because, you see, he loved his wife too.

I asked him more about his earlier life. He told me of his father, a successful businessman, who preferred his brother to him. He told me how his father had no use for him, how he had ridiculed him all his life, how his father had downgraded his ability and belittled everything he tried to do.

Resentful, he had left his father's place of business, where he had been employed, and got a job as a salesman. He made out fairly well as a salesman, well enough to support his wife and child, anyway. But he continued to seethe with resentment at his rejecting father; he could not get his father out of his mind for long. He, too, could not rise above the hatefulness of his past.

Still, he lived a fairly decent life—holding his own as a salesman, husband and father. Until, in his sleep, semi-conscious, he found himself trying to choke his wife—and tortured himself with the knowledge of what he had almost done. In this tortured state, fantasying further attempts at unleashing his resentment so destructively, he came to see me.

Two men, so alike and yet so different. Self-torturing, denying themselves self-respect, the fires of resentment destroying them from within.

"But why not?" you may say. "Look at their backgrounds. They were hurt. Why shouldn't they feel resentment?"

True, why shouldn't they? They were hurt; no one can deny this. The man with the smothering mother was badly hurt; so was the man with the rejecting father.

But if you stop here you are missing my point, which is this: How do we help them? By encouraging them in nursing their feeling of deprivation and thereby helping them stoke the furnace of resentment?

I think not. But, before I tell what I said to them and how I feel about their potential adjustment to life, let me tell you about a formerly fat taxi driver who won out over his resentment.

One Victory Over Resentment

I boarded a taxi at Kennedy Airport. I was tired and closed my eyes but the cabbie was talkative and told me a story of one victory over resentment.

"Where you coming from?" he asked.

"Los Angeles."

"It must be hot out there."

"So-so."

"It's been cold here. What's your business?"

"I'm a doctor."

"A doctor! Boy, do I need a doctor!"

"You do?"

"Yeah, didn't you notice how fat I am? You know how much I weigh? Two hundred fifty-five pounds."

"Why don't you try to reduce?"

He held up a paper bag. "See this. Half a chicken and some pot cheese. That's my diet."

"Does it help?"

"It did. I lost thirty pounds but then I get depressed and angry, and I start eating a lot again."

"What's the matter?"

"Well, I get mad."

"What about?"

"Would you be interested?"

"Yes."

"Oh you would not, buddy. I'm a hopeless case, I guess."

"Are you married?"

"I was. I got married when I was very young. I have two kids, both boys, sixteen and seventeen."

"Were you so fat then?"

"Yeah, but she loved me anyway. At least she seemed to at first."

"So?"

"She began talking about how she was ashamed of me because I was so fat. I figured she was right, so I went on a diet. I ate pot cheese and chicken all the time. I lost over thirty pounds."

"Good."

"No, it was no good. I thought that when I looked thinner my wife would be happier with me, but it didn't work out that way. Something was wrong. You know, you can tell when a woman likes you, she doesn't have to say anything, just the way she looks at you. Well, I'd look at her and see something was wrong. She had this faraway look."

"What then?"

"I went to see my best friend. I've known him for many years. He said he would straighten things out; he told me not to worry."

"Did he?"

"Oh sure. You've heard the story before—nothing new. I found them together in bed one day. I don't know what stopped me from killing him. I could have choked her too. I felt like it. Instead, I ran out of the house, got into my taxi and drove. And drove. And drove. I drove for two days, till I hit Florida. I felt so mad, that was all I could think to do."

"I'm sorry," I said, "about what happened. Guess you're divorced now?"

"Yeah, sure. She married him. I felt sorry for her."

"And for yourself? Don't you feel sorry for yourself?"

"Sure. Look at me, driving around with a paper bag full of chicken and pot cheese. Why am I trying to get thin? For whom?"

"You're doing it for yourself."

"I hate myself," he said. "I hate them. Maybe I hate almost everybody."

"Be responsible to yourself," I said. "Lose weight so you'll feel better about yourself. That's the main thing."

"I don't know."

"I know it's not easy, but you've got to get over your resentment and regain your self-respect. Lose weight. Stop feeling sorry for yourself. Look, here's my card. I dare you to come see me when you are thin."

It was about a year later, and there he was in my office. I had trouble recognizing him. He looked like a different person. All the fat was gone; he couldn't have weighed much more than 160 or 170 pounds. And, biggest change of all, there was a broad smile on his face.

"I did it," he said.

"I'm happy for you," I said. "You look fine."

"I feel fine."

"You look like you won out over your anger."

"I won," he said.

"Will you ever get married again?"

"I did," he said. "I did that too. She's a beauty. I'm crazy about her. Here's a picture of her."

One victory over resentment. From fat to thin, change one. The biggest change: from resentment to happiness.

A Positive Approach to Resentment

So, now, let us put our heads together and plan a positive approach toward resentment. To find self-respect, you must find in yourself the weapons to use against the negation of resentment—and, to define my terms more precisely, what I mean is "chronic resentment."

First, you must disabuse yourself of any idea that you are alone when you feel resentment. Everyone feels resentful sometimes because everyone, at one time or another, experiences frustration, grief, disappointment, and despair. The distinction is this: The person who lacks self-respect stays resentful, fails to get over it, inflicts his hostility on others; the person with self-respect climbs out of the pit, gets over it, goes on to a constructive life of which he can be proud.

Now, what do you do?

Well, first, let's go back to the two men I wrote about. They were so resentful that (in different ways) each kept fantasizing choking—or being choked—to death.

What did I say to them?

Well, the first man had, I felt, been especially unfortunate in being so smothered by his mother, and of course I understood his resentment and his fear. His mother, perhaps fearing another desertion, kept him by her side and thus blocked his growth as a person. Indeed, you might say that she used him as a substitute for the husband who had deserted her.

So, in his early formative years, this man had been deserted by his father and imprisoned by his mother. Good God, why shouldn't he feel resentment? I thought, but I didn't say this.

Because resentment was no solution for his problems. Feeling resentment as he moved out into the world, he would get resentment back from others and would spend his life in a never-ending cycle of negation, a death-in-life cycle of misery. Obviously, his early experiences would limit what he could do with his life; still, this did not mean that he could not, within limits, lead a good life.

"I cannot blame you," I said, "for feeling resentment toward both your parents. Don't feel guilty if you feel this way. But, at the same time, recognize that it won't do you any good and that you must change your ways of thinking."

"How?" he said.

"You have had some good moments in your life, too," I said. "You just told me about some of them. Think about them, not about your mother, bring them into the present. Feel these successes now. Live now. Set your goals today. Set them every day."

"I'm not sure I have any goals," he said. "And if I did, they wouldn't be important anyway."

"They would be important," I said. "If you set a goal, say, of approaching a customer in a positive way or stopping your critical thoughts about yourself, I would call either an important goal. A very important goal."

"But what about my mother?" he said.

"If all you can feel is resentment when you think of your mother, live in the present and don't think about her too much. Concentrate on defeating your resentment and accepting yourself and going toward goals that will make you feel good about yourself. Someday maybe you'll forgive your mother—when you feel better about yourself, maybe you will feel compassion for her failings. When you are able to think this way about her, without resentment, then think more about her. I hope that someday you will forgive yourself—and forgive your mother, too."

What about the second man?

"As far as I can see," I said, "you are so full of resentment toward your father that you transfer this feeling—almost unconsciously, perhaps—to your wife and, though you do love her, in your ambivalence you fantasy choking her and found yourself almost doing that very thing.

"You must understand this: You cannot be responsible for your father's belittling attitude toward you. You don't have to see him all the time if you don't want to. You don't work for him anymore. So why the continual resentment?"

"I can't help it," he said. "Look what he did to me."

"You have a good job, a wife, a child," I said. "You have problems, I can see, but you have good solid qualities too. Maybe your father was far from perfect, but he did not destroy you. Build a new life for yourself.

"Forget your father, forgive your father. Live for today, without resentment destroying your day. You are more than your father thinks you are. You are what you think you are. Forgive yourself for what you almost did; accept yourself, get over your resentment, set new goals. You have fine goals to set, a rich life to lead, a good marriage to build—if you will forgive yourself and your father and get over the resentment that burns inside you like a cancer."

Postscript: Months later, the man phoned to tell me of the improvements in his life. There were no more choking fantasies or near-attempts. He was earning more money and enjoying his work. His wife and he were feeling closer and reexperiencing their natural affection for each other. His child was thriving. He saw his father seldom, but no longer felt submerged in his resentment toward him.

The first man I have not heard from. He has much to overcome. I hope he succeeds.

I have indicated my idea of a positive approach to resentment in my advice to these men. But let me summarize this advice:

1. Rise above the deprivations of your past. This is not easy, but neither is bathing yourself in self-pity and hate.

2. Set goals every day. You are worth it. Your goals are important if they are important to you. Stop turning your resentment in on yourself. Move toward your goals instead.

3. Forgive others. Anyway, try. Have other people let you down? Try to forgive them anyway. They are not perfect; you are not perfect. Forgiveness is the soothing balm that takes away resentment.

4. Forgive yourself. Forgive yourself every day. When you let others down, when you let yourself down, forgive yourself. I have made my mistakes, and you have made your mistakes. Forgive!

And overcome the fallacious concept you may have—many people do—about the heroism and "guts" of expressing resentment in a belligerent way. There is nothing heroic about lashing out at other people with destruction and there is no "guts" in using as a model some renowned tough guy criminal who ended up in jail or incorrigibly alienated from society. It amazes me sometimes that so many people admire these anti-social types in their hard-bitten and negative resentment.

The person with real "guts" is a big enough person to rise above his resentment, to adopt a constructive way of life, to contribute all he can to other people, to reach out—in his imperfection, in his all-too-human imperfection—toward life with the best he has in him.

This kind of person has felt resentment and has even been submerged in resentment, but he has won the battle to overcome it. He has won this great battle. He does not have to show off and prove that he has "guts." Deep down inside, he knows that he does.

He feels self-respect. He bestows this great gift on himself. When he looks in the mirror, he may chuckle a little—but he does not cry and he does not flinch and he is not in pain.

This is the gift you must give yourself: self-respect.

CHAPTER 6

Your Third Enemy: Emptiness

YOU are on the road to self-respect. Your car is sleek, the gas tank is full, the highway is firm. There are no detours; your direction is forward.

You harness the supercharged powers in your understanding and in your feeling of active sincerity. These are awesome powers; do not doubt this. They are subtle and positive powers that will lead you toward a good feeling about yourself and others—fundamental components of any self-respectful orientation in this our complicated twentieth-century world.

Thus, when we win out over the negative and self-destructive forces in ourselves—the uncertainty and the resentment—we then call on our positive capacities to build our sense of human dignity, to move us toward our goals, to make the most of our lives.

Before we go on to a consideration of more positive aspects leading to your sense of self-respect, let us learn about your third enemy: emptiness.

Like resentment and uncertainty, this is a dread enemy. Perhaps it is man's greatest enemy these days. Because of my extensive travels and lectures, I talk to a pretty fair cross section of people. Not every one can articulate what is bothering him, but a common thread runs through what I hear. Many people today suffer from a constant sense of incompleteness, of non-being—of what I would call emptiness.

This may seem strange to you: That in a land of material plenty, in an era which economic indexes herald as a time of unparalleled prosperity, so many people should feel so empty. That living as we do, well fed, well clothed, whisking around in cars and jets, so many people should feel an internal lack. That in an era of rising personal incomes, rising savings, and rising participation in ownership of such tangibles as shares of stock, so many people should wonder who they are and spend their days in a fruitless and often bizarre search for identity.

And yet it is so. Too many people have passively withdrawn from life and from themselves, cut themselves off from the glow of their creative powers, and turned their eyes toward externals in an effort to fill the void of their emptiness. They seek to erase this inner lack by turning to alcohol or drugs, indulging in excesses of food or entertainment, or trying to identify with the lives of celebrities.

But this is not the way to take away emptiness. In the final analysis, *you* must give yourself substance and *you* must overcome your sense of emptiness yourself. This is your responsibility to yourself, your joy in doing, your sense of accomplishment when you succeed.

If a sense of emptiness haunts you, you must win out over this third enemy. First is uncertainty; then, resentment, and finally, emptiness. These are the principal negative forces that stand between you and the full sense of self-respect that you deserve to feel.

When I was a boy, we used to hear other kids (usually a

year or two older, and braggarts all) talk about the horrifying "haunted house" in the neighborhood. Remember?

Sometimes we would walk past this "haunted house" and look at it with a peculiar mixture of curiosity and fear—keeping a respectful distance, of course, and crossing our fingers or some such nonsense.

Finally, prodded on by curiosity and an effort to show how brave we were, we gathered up our courage, launched ourselves piously into prayer, and crossed the threshold.

To discover . . . what?

To discover that the house was just an ordinary house—no "ghosts" at all—just empty.

My point is that we must learn to do away with our childish haunted-house-type illusions—they are empty. We must be strong enough to live in and to face the solid world of a reality.

Further, we must rebuild ourselves from the ground up, so that our foundations are strong. Insight is our window; inner peace, our furniture; and the excitement of our goals, the fuel for heating. Thus we build ourselves, become strong persons, and overcome the despair of emptiness.

Emptiness and Fulfillment

Before I give you my ideas on dealing with emptiness more concretely, I will tell you three short stories about people I know. These people are of my world, and of your world, too—for their problems may be your problems and their anguish may be your anguish.

The first is about a man who came up to speak to me after a lecture in Florida. He was a big, heavy-set man and he talked to me about his feeling of emptiness and his lack of trust in people—including his wife and three children.

"This emptiness, this lack of trust—maybe it came from the war," he said.

He had been in the infantry in Europe in World War II and more than once he had killed other men. "Maybe that's why I feel so bad," he said.

"I doubt it," I said. "You were fighting for your country and you were forced to either kill or be killed yourself."

Then he told me about his childhood. How he was the least favored of his family. His parents thought him worthless, and he grew up with a poor feeling about himself.

"There's where your problem comes from, probably," I said, "from the poor opinion of yourself that has stayed with you from your childhood. You still believe what your parents thought of you. This empty feeling, this bad feeling, you cannot win over it until you learn to live today, in the present, to forgive yourself for what is not your fault—to set goals for today."

Here is another story. It is about a couple who married and divorced. About emptiness, several years of emptiness.

They came to see me after one of my lectures and told me about themselves. They had remarried. Both had read my book *Psycho-Cybernetics*—separately—and had learned to stop hating each other and start forgiving. Their sense of emptiness, mixed up in this resentment, grew less and less. Finally, they decided to forgive each other for all their grudges in marriage and they began to think of the good times they had shared.

They thanked me for writing my book.

How did I feel when they told me this? How would you feel if someone walked up to you on the street and handed you a million dollars.

Another story came singing to me over the phone, three

years ago, spanning the thousands of miles between New York and Texas.

"I did it."

"What?" I said.

"I did it."

I looked at the telephone. What a funny instrument it was, I thought.

"It worked," said the voice booming over the telephone. "It worked."

I was in my office. I had just finished operating. My mind and body were both just a little tired. "Who is this?" I managed to ask.

"Don't you remember me?" The voice roared out of the telephone out at me. "I drove you to the airport and I told you about me and my son."

"Oh," I said.

"I'm the salesman from Texas. The guy who made a lot of money talking to other people, who couldn't talk to his son."

"How are you?" I said. "I'm glad to hear from you."

"It worked," he said.

"Oh," I said.

"I did it," he said.

"Congratulations," I said.

"It worked," he said.

"Great. But, I'm kind of tired, please forgive me—what worked? What did you do?"

He reminded me of what he'd talked to me about—the great emptiness in his life, his inability to communicate with his son.

The emptiness of it! He was making a good living, he had a fine teenage son—but he couldn't reach hm.

He was driving me to the airport; I had to catch a plane

and didn't have much time. "Talk to him," I had said. "Even if it's difficult—and painful. If you've failed him in any ways, ask his forgiveness. Tell him something like this: 'Son, forgive me. I may have made a mistake about you, but isn't it possible that you've also made a mistake about me?' "

Behind the steering wheel his face was full of despair. He had nodded his head, but he seemed empty to me.

I had advised him some more—on forgiveness of himself, and of his son, and on making a fresh start—and then we had shaken hands goodbye.

Now here he was, materialized from out of this little miracle gadget we take for granted. "It worked," he said.

"What happened?" I said.

"I stopped being so proud," he said. "I humbled myself. I forgave myself, I forgave him—and I couldn't believe the way he reacted. We embraced. We cried. He became the son I used to be close to. My son and I are close again."

"I'm happy for you."

It was three years ago when this man had phoned me to tell me of his victory over emptiness and to thank me. I had talked about him to people, here and there, and written about him a little, too.

Then just the other day, as I was writing this book, I picked up the telephone and there he was again.

"I want you to know, Max," he said, "that as I travel around the country I keep hearing the story of me and my son."

"My lectures," I said. "I like to talk about you."

"I'm glad you're telling my story," he said. "I hope it helps other people. My son and I are closer today than ever. We have been the best of friends since I talked to him in a humble way—finally."

"You did it," I said.

"What?"

"It worked," I said.

"What?"

"You did it," I said.

"You're kidding," he said.

"I am. But I'm laughing with you, that you let down your pride and found your human dignity, that you won out over your emptiness. This is something to laugh about. It is something to feel happy about. People don't laugh enough these days; they have to learn how to laugh."

"Thanks," he said.

"I talk too much," I said. "But call me again."

Three stories about people who I have helped feel less empty. And they have helped me feel more fulfilled. Inded, I do not tell of them to show how they are in my debt; for, most assuredly, *I am in their debt*. I tell these stories of people grappling with emptiness because emptiness is one of the prime obstacles to the attainment of our sense of self-respect.

Twentieth-Century Emptiness

Do you suffer from a feeling of emptiness?

If you do, take heart; you are not alone. You are one of many people wrestling with one of the dread diseases of the twentieth century. To reach up to your full feeling of dignity, you must overcome this emptiness.

Too many people wake up to feelings of aimlessness, substancelessness, and go to face days which lack meaning and a sense of direction.

Too many people today suffer from a kind of twentieth-century emptiness—with excuses for their voids, endless complaints for anyone who will listen, and a mañana philosophy underlying and poisoning their lives.

Some people think they feel empty because they are not married; but this need not be so. Some people think they feel empty because they have no children; but this need not be so. Others believe their emptiness stems from the fact that they are not overwhelming successes in their work; but this need not be so.

You create your own feeling of emptiness, to a great degree, and *you* must accept responsibility for overcoming it.

In reality—not fantasy.

Too many people wish they were somebody else.

When you wake up in the morning, do you say to yourself, "If I only had a million dollars"?

I hope not. Because if you do, you are licked before you start. You are rejecting yourself as you are, leaving yourself empty and unfulfilled.

Or perhaps you say to yourself, "If only I were a beautiful Hollywood actress."

Again, I hope not. I might add, I have known beautiful Hollywood actresses who wished that they were somebody else too.

Or maybe you think, "If only I was twenty years younger."

You were twenty years younger once. What did you do with your youth when you had it?

Stop wishing you were somebody else; start enjoying the unique privilege of being yourself. Wishing is an evasion— and it leads you only to despair.

I used to know a man many people would consider fortunate—because he was extremely wealthy. He and his brother owned a number of business enterprises years ago;

they had amassed a considered sum of money—or so I was led to believe.

Still, he was always bored. He found little to interest himself. He suffered from an enormous sense of indifference.

There were hordes of nice girls in New York, but he went to the south of France to meet a countess whom he would marry. With him he took a sense of emptiness and illusion, and he fell into the hands of some people who played games with him and tricked him. A fake baron introduced him to a fake countess and her daughter, both of whom fawned on him—and he was blissfully unaware of the manipulations going on around him.

To the best of my knowledge, he emerged from all this unscathed. I hope so, anyway. He was really a decent fellow. But he suffered from a terrible sense of emptiness that drove him into such illusion and made him a target for such confidence people.

Do you think you wouldn't feel empty and bored if you had a lot of money? Here was someone who had a lot of money—and he still felt an appalling emptiness.

Now, what do we do about this? How do we fill ourselves so that we no longer feel empty? How do we discard all our elaborate excuses and get down to brass tacks?

Five Ways to Vanquish Emptiness

Here are some suggestions I have to give you. I think they may help you.

1. Stop sleepwalking. Approximately eight hours a day you should sleep and sleep soundly—you need sleep to renew your energy and bring you back to yourself.

When you are awake, stay awake. Concentrate on what

you are doing; stop doing things halfheartedly. If some project is important enough for you to undertake it, throw yourself into it with concentration and enthusiasm and with your full life force.

Will all this exhaust you?

Not at all. Concentration is a fine art; in sharpening your focus on the things that interest you, you become more fully alive and this is exhilarating. Instead of sleepwalking, you will live more while you are awake and chances are you will then also sleep more soundly and wake up, not exhausted, but refreshed.

The sleepwalker feels empty because he just wanders around in a daze and does nothing. Stop sleepwalking, make your activities purposeful, fill your days with vitality.

2. Resign from Mañana Incorporated. I have written about this bankrupt corporation in some of my other books, but just a few more words about it in connection with emptiness.

Members of Mañana Incorporated—addicted to the tomorrow-type thinking—put off everything until mañana [tomorrow]. Thus they never realize their goals because they always delay going after them until a "mañana" that no one I know has ever even experienced.

Members of Mañana Incorporated never get any dividends. They are in the business of rationalizing why they cannot do something today, but must put it off until "tomorrow." They live fiercely in the future, disdaining to dirty their hands with the sordidness of the present.

The result of all this?

Emptiness, of course.

Because they never do anything.

So, you millions of members of Mañana Incorporated, do yourselves a favor and resign.

3. Renew your sense of direction. Because you cannot go around in endless circles. If you do this, obviously you get a listless, aimless, indifferent kind of feeling about your life.

Yet many people do just this—and see nothing wrong with their lifeless, empty orientation.

Suppose you boarded an airplane which left New York, whisked over Philadelphia, circled back to New York, changed direction and jet-propelled itself to Chicago, then moved toward Canada, only to circle back to Chicago and then back to New York, where it did not land but continued to circle for hours, until it moved again toward Philadelphia.

"Ridiculous!" you say. "What kind of an airplane is this? An airplane that goes nowhere. Absurd!"

Truly, an airplane with no sense of direction is a horrifying thing to contemplate. But what about a person who has no sense of direction? Is this not also a terrible waste?

Of course. Just as boarding an airplane which does nothing but go around in circles is an experience in emptiness, so an individual who spends his precious time going around in circles lives with emptiness.

You must renew your sense of direction to break through the feeling of emptiness and give valid meaning to your life. Every day set your goals. Don't downgrade them; give them your full enthusiasm. You deserve to feel that the goals that are important to you are worthwhile. So you won't make a million dollars. So your name won't be in the headlines. It doesn't matter. What does matter is that your goals mean something to you. What does matter is that your zest for them helps you lift yourself up out of your feeling of empty nothingness into a feeling of doing something and being somebody. No one else has to sanction that you are somebody either; this is something that you give yourself.

4. Enrich your self-image. When you have a good opinion of yourself, when you use your imagination productively, you enrich your self-image and you dissolve the empty, negative feeling you have about yourself.

You have already seen too much of your failures; seeing your failures again and again in your mind has produced only negation and has engendered in you a sense that you are empty and inferior—lacking in worth as a human being.

See your successes instead! Your imagination has enormous power, and can help you picture your successes and bring enrichment to your self-image.

I have said this before, in other books, but I cannot possibly repeat it too much—it is too fundamental: When you see your successes in your imagination instead of your failures, you precondition yourself for more and more success, for a reactivation of your success mechanism. In the process you enrich your self-image and move out into the world with a confidence that is reality, not overcompensation or fantasy.

As you enrich your self-image, it goes almost without saying, you dissolve your feeling of emptiness.

5. Reach out to other people. This, too, is fundamental and just as, in a sense, you dissolve emptiness as you enrich your self-image, so you also dissolve emptiness as you reach out— in a constructive way—toward other people.

And this is the common denominator I had in mind when telling the stories of five people fighting to win out over their feelings of emptiness. Their feelings of emptiness or of fulfillment had much to do with their ability or their lack of ability to reach out and communicate successfully with other people.

One man feared closeness with his family—he did not

trust them—but he was probably well off the mark when he blamed this on his killing enemy soldiers during the war.

The couple, who felt able to forgive and forget were able to overcome their sense of emptiness and reach out toward each other once more.

The father and son, too, were able to bury their past grievances, were able to feel a warm bond again and, as they did, fulfillment replaced emptiness.

In short, to win out over emptiness, material achievements are not enough. You must value more than the material; you must reach out with friendship to people.

People values: sharing with people; living on friendly terms with them; and loving. These are the values that will bring you fulfillment instead of emptiness.

Our Final Goal: Self-Respect

Our final goal is self-respect and, moving toward this goal, we have examined a trio of deadly enemies that might block our path toward our goals. These enemies are negative feelings: uncertainty, resentment, emptiness. They are invisible, but they are dread enemies nevertheless.

We have devoted a chapter to each of these possible pitfalls because stressing positive concepts is not enough if we do not have an awareness of the negative forces inside us.

A friend of mine who was a soldier in World War II told me a story which is illustrative. He was an infantryman, a squad leader, and his outfit was fighting the Germans door-to-door in a town near the German border.

One night, after midnight, his platoon went on patrol behind the German lines. They crawled through the snow to a house at the end of a block and my friend was told he was to lead the charge. He did, rushing across a barbed-wire-strewn mine field, to the house across the street. A German sentry guarding the entrance fled and, after hurling grenades in the house, the GIs rushed in. Four Germans waited in the cellar, surrendering hands over head while they were searched.

But the soldiers were not completely vigilant—or they were too excited or frightened—and the fourth German was not searched (or handcuffed or tied). To my friend's horror, this German soldier reached over to hand him two grenades with which he could have wreaked fearful destruction. He handed him the grenades; he could as easily have hurled them in his face.

The patrol was a success. The platoon returned with the four prisoners, who faced interrogation at headquarters.

But what might have been! Because the American soldiers had not coped properly with the enemy, their mission might have been a disastrous failure.

Our mission is self-respect and, before moving full force on it, we too must search out our negative forces and take away the destructive grenades before they can explode and ruin our mission.

We cannot keep moving forward toward self-respect while we are arming our negative forces of uncertainty, resentment, and emptiness.

We cannot build and face destruction at the same time.

But now we know a good deal about the negative forces inside us and we will resume our positive emphases.

We know our rights; we will not short-change ourselves; we will seize our opportunities to build for ourselves lives of solid human dignity.

CHAPTER 7

Developing the Strength
to Seize Opportunities

WHAT is opportunity, and when does it knock? It never knocks. You can wait a whole lifetime, listening, hoping, and you will hear no knocking. None at all.

You are opportunity, and you must knock on the door leading to your destiny. You prepare yourself to recognize opportunity, to pursue and seize opportunity as you develop the strength of your personality and build a self-image with which you are able to live—with your self-respect alive and growing.

Opportunity covers a wide area: some people may constrict the totality of its meaning and apply it only to work or financial success, but your opportunities in living are really much wider than this. Opportunity may also mean warding off negative feelings. It may also mean functioning under pressure. It may also mean rising above vanity, bigotry, and deceit as you strive to live with dignity. It is your opportunity to be an archaeologist digging under the debris of tension and conflict to uncover for yourself a sense of self-acceptance that will give you inner peace and comfort in our swiftly paced, always troubled world.

Accessible to you may be the exciting opportunity of steering yourself to a productive goal through your growing awareness of who you are and what you can be and how you can channel your assets in practical terms toward achieving your ends. Developing your strength as you build your self-respect, you mobilize yourself for action and place yourself—practically, in an external sense, and emotionally, in an internal sense—in a position to seize opportunities at the proper times. You build the caliber of your thinking, propelling your thoughts into and through your imagination. Then with internal strength, you move toward your goals of fulfillment and happiness.

You create opportunity. *You* develop the capacities for moving toward opportunity. *You* turn crises into creative opportunities and defeats into successes and frustration into fulfillment.

With what? With your great invisible weapons: your good feelings about yourself, your determination to live the best life you can, and your feeling—that only you can give yourself—that you are a worthwhile, deserving person.

You must fight for your right to fulfill the opportunity that God gave you to use your life well. You do this when, in your mind, you support yourself instead of undermining yourself. You do this when, in your mind, you develop your creative and imaginative powers instead of worrying about what other people think or foreseeing endless disasters.

What are explorers? Men alive to opportunity and adventure. Men unafraid to challenge uncertainty and seek new horizons. Men alive to possibilities of expansion and innovation. Suppose, in 1492, Columbus had said to himself, "But the weather may be stormy" or "I'd better not go. I might get scurvy."

What are inventors? Men who see opportunity in things where others see none. Men whose senses are alive to creative possibilities. Where would the world be today if Thomas Edison had been unable to see opportunity where others saw nothing—and then to seize it?

You must stop complaining about your unfortunate past or your bad luck and open your eyes to the opportunities that exist for you. You have limitations, sure, and no matter who you are, you will sometimes meet frustrations—but you have opportunities too, and you must search for your creative powers so that you can move toward them. In a sense, you become Columbus, you become Edison; you explore and invent and originate and adapt.

Who gives you this right? You give it to yourself because you respect yourself.

Opportunity Is Not Just for the Other Guy

From New York to California, I have gone back and forth lecturing for quite a few years now, and I have talked to thousands of people about things that worry them—so let me anticipate a few thoughts of many people reading this:

"The other guy gets opportunities. I know that. But I'm just unlucky."

Or "I have this handicap, so you can see that I'm licked before I start."

Or "I have no right to try something like that. Who am I, just a nobody."

This is self-defeating; you must fight to overcome this type of negative thinking or you block yourself off from opportunity as an eclipse blocks off the sun.

You must understand that opportunity is not just for "the other guy." Opportunity is a possibility for you, too—if you can accept it and make it welcome. A plant may wither and die if you don't water it and give it enough sunshine. So will opportunity.

Don't let opportunity die for you! Don't kill it with negative feelings!

There is much concern in education today about "disadvantaged" children in our schools and in many communities university teams are helping public school teachers to improve communication between school, students and parents and thereby to get the "disadvantaged" children more of a chance to climb up the educational and vocational ladder.

Well, as adults, we all have disadvantages—and limitations. If we get help—as these children are getting today—wonderful. If we don't, we must nevertheless move toward whatever opportunities are realistic for us anyway.

Many people sit around moping, envying others, complaining, resentful. If they hear about people like Helen Keller, who overcame drastic handicaps to seize her opportunities for achievement, they say that this is an isolated case.

Indeed, in the case of Helen Keller, her handicaps were so severe that perhaps she is an isolated case.

Still, in general, many people who have pursued and seized their opportunities and risen to prominent positions in our world have had no easy road.

A study was made of four hundred eminent men and women of this century, and the researchers concluded that three-fourths of these celebrated people had been handicapped in their youth by tragedies, disabilities, or great frustrations and had overcome these problems to achieve their position of renown and make their contributions to others. Three-fourths of these four hundred people fought through their handicaps; an important statistic. Thomas Edison and Eleanor Roosevelt were included among those who had risen above handicaps to achievement and opportunity.

Opportunity is not just for others. But you must make opportunity for you.

Don't Close the Door on Opportunity!

Opportunity won't knock on your door; nevertheless you must not close the door on opportunity.

Apply creative psycho-cybernetics, and rise to meet opportunity, forgiving yourself for your failures and continually moving toward new goals.

To close the door on opportunity is, unfortunately, common. You must guard against this type of tendency in yourself. Let me tell you an illustrative story:

It's about a doctor who shut the door on an opportunity to advance himself.

He was already a doctor; and he wanted to become a plastic surgeon.

"Can I watch you operate?" he asked me.

"Tomorrow," I said. "Eight A.M. Okay?"

I wasn't sure the "eight A.M." pleased him, but I figured I was probably imagining this. He nodded his head. "I'll be there," he said. "Eight A.M."

He was as good as his word. He was there at eight A.M. and he watched me operate. He said he was fascinated. Could he be my pupil? I agreed that I would teach him.

The doctor came a few times, expressing fascination with plastic surgery and for the opportunity for fulfillment that this work could be for him.

I was delighted with his enthusiasm.

But one morning he was not there.

The morning after that he was also absent.

Finally, a few days later, I walked into my office and there he was. "Where have you been?" I said.

"I overslept a few times," he answered, rather sheepishly. "When I woke up, I looked at the time and it was too late to come."

"You won't learn this way," I said mildly.

"I know. Tell me, do you operate in the afternoon? I like to sleep, and it would be easier for me."

"Sorry. I always operate in the morning. The patient has just awakened, and I feel it is best for the patient psychologically."

"Oh," he said.

And, fascinated as he was with plastic surgery (it represented a creative opportunity for him, and I do not believe he faked his interest) he didn't follow up. He couldn't get up early in the morning. He shut the door on his own opportunity. He was qualified to succeed, but he denied himself success in his own terms.

Learn from this story. Are you, without knowing it, blocking yourself from opportunity? You have this great gift of life, and you must make the most of it. When you fail—and sometimes you will—let it be after you have done your best, not as a result of your own inertia.

Now let me tell you a story about a scrubwoman who found opportunity.

A Song of Happiness

I met her, this scrubwoman, in the elevator one evening. I had enjoyed my dinner in a nearby restaurant, returned home about eight o'clock, and stepped into the elevator to go up to the eighteenth floor, where I live. She was armed with mop and pail. A small woman, in her late forties, she had worked about ten years in the building, but we didn't know each other any better than to nod our heads and say hello. That's what we did this night: we nodded our heads, and murmured "hello."

She came up with me to my place, with mop and pail, ready to empty the wastepaper basket and mop the floors. While she started on a front room, I walked to the living room.

I made myself comfortable. I was smoking my pipe, my feet were up, I was reading a play. I had forgotten about the scrubwoman's presence. She might have been on another planet.

Then I heard singing from another room—no, humming. Someone was humming a lullaby. It was soft and sweet and happy-sounding, a song of happiness.

I got out of my chair. In another room the woman was mopping the floor, humming her lullaby. She looked up as I entered the room and we exchanged greetings again.

"Did you have a busy day?" she asked me.

"Yes. And you?"

"About the same as usual."

"But today is different, isn't it?"

"How?"

"You're smiling, and you're humming a song."

"I often do. It makes my work more pleasant. I'm cleaning up, and I'm singing while I work, so I'm happy."

"I never heard you before," I said.

"Perhaps not."

"And," I said, "we never talked before."

"That's true."

I asked her about herself. Her life had been a difficult one —enough to crush many an individual who could not endure grief and rise above it to regain herself. Her husband, a truck driver for the government, had been killed in a car accident twelve years earlier. She had one child, a daughter—nine at the time of the accident—now twenty-one, unmarried, a college girl. She and her daughter were in the car with her husband when it crashed and he died; by some miracle the woman and her daughter had survived.

Grief stricken at her husband's sudden and horrible death, consoling her daughter who at such a young age had seen such a frightening tragedy and suffered such a catastrophic loss, she had nevertheless found in herself the courage to go on. She had for many years supported herself and her daughter, who was soon to graduate from college in Wisconsin.

"What will she do then?" I asked her.

"She majored in psychology. She'll go for her master's degree and then she's going to get a job teaching underprivileged children."

"May I congratulate you?"

"Do you want to?"

"I do. I think you deserve it. I think you should be very proud of yourself."

"I am proud."

"You should be."

"And I'm happy."

"Good."

"About my daughter."

"That's fine," I said. "But I feel also that you should be proud of your great achievement—of the way you came through for your daughter when she was a little girl and you didn't let her down."

"Thanks, doctor."

"You know, we've never talked before—all these years—but I've seen you now and then and you look different somehow. What is it?"

"My wig?"

"Oh." I looked at her hair. "Oh. That's it. Yes."

"Do you like it?" She was suddenly shy, almost a little sensitive; in a flash, she seemed waiting, depending on my opinion, hoping for my approval.

"I like it."

"Does it make me look like a lady?"

"You always were." I hate to flatter people, but I felt an honest respect for her that made me enjoy complimenting her.

She stood there with mop and pail, her eyes gleaming with pleasure. No princess or countess on the French Riviera ever gleamed with more inner pride. "I wanted to look better for my daughter. I'm so proud of what she's learning and what she's planning to do with her life. She wants to contribute to the children of the world—she is sincere in this—and then she wants to have children of her own and teach them to lead useful lives and to assume responsibility as human beings."

I went back into the other room to continue my reading; strange, all these years, coming and going, nodding hello as people whose lives meet on no level at all—and suddenly I knew so much about the woman who scrubbed my floors and cleaned up. Some people might look down on her because they thought her work demeaning: I could only respect her for her courage in rising above misfortune and maintaining her self-respect in the face of a tragedy that would have crushed many people.

Humming again, soft and sweet. Happy. A song of happiness from a scrubwoman. She wore a wig to cover her hair, but she needed no artificial aid to cover her sense of purpose. It was there.

Husband alive, husband dead—just like that—but she had overcome her grief and terror to find opportunity once more. Still, she had reached out to find opportunity in helping her daughter toward a life hopefully easier than her own had been.

Even while working—tiring, painstaking, ill-rewarded work—she found opportunity to sing a song of happiness.

How to Move Toward Opportunity

This world is far from perfect—you don't have to be brilliant to perceive that—but it nevertheless contains many opportunities for fulfillment and achievement.

Some people spend all their time criticizing the American culture and, while some of their criticism may be quite valid, still we must be pragmatists. We must ask: "Where have men grouped together in civilizations and behaved like angels, with absolute justice and absolute constructive effort and absolute brotherhood and peace of mind?"

Even ancient Athens, home of so many great philosophers whose thoughts have lived through the ages, even ancient Athens had serious defects as a culture. The worst of which was its lack of an adequate sanitary system. The lack of a sanitary system helped spread a terrible plague which was largely instrumental in destroying ancient Athens.

All right, we live in an imperfect world, in an imperfect culture, and as you settle in your easy chair after a hard day's work to read your newspaper all the frightening headlines upset you further and finally, thoroughly irritated, you throw the newspaper at your cat. But the cat slinks away. Even the cat doesn't want to read about all the world's troubles.

Yet ours is a world of opportunity, too. The frontiers are not all closed, and the doors are not all shut. We can still look forward and move forward—toward exciting new opportunities.

How?

1. Keep an eye on the red light. I mean the red light on your mental dashboard, with which you stop yourself from moving toward your opportunities. Red lights on our streets are necessary for safety, of course. But when you stop yourself, you must ask yourself this: Am I stopping myself for realistic reasons, because I am moving into a danger area, or am I just stopping myself because my opinion of myself is too low, and I do not believe I deserve success?

Stop wasting fuel worrying about yesterday. Just as you would take care of your car, oil it, and check it out—take care of your emotional car, so that it moves you toward your objectives.

Stop when the red light on your mental dashboard signals a necessary slowdown—but change it to green when, for no real reason except negative feelings, you would keep yourself from moving forward down the main highway toward opportunity.

Stop and start—this is the way to move toward your goals.

As you formulate them and move toward them, remember your past successes and, even more important, see them in your mind as if they were happening *now*. Thus your success lives again, in your imagination, so that you live and breathe the success of the past and project it into the present, thus pouring psycho-cybernetic oil into the creative engine of your mind.

Stop, but then start again.

2. *Live in the present*. The past is gone; the future is unknown—but the present is real, and your opportunities are now. You must see these opportunities; they must be real for you.

The catch is that they can't seem real if your mind is buried in past failures, if you keep reliving old mistakes, old guilts, old tragedies.

Creative psycho-cybernetics means that you focus on goals today and use the past only to sharpen your success feelings as you move toward your goals. You forgive yourself for your mistakes and your failures and you take a friendly look at yourself and understand that you must stop torturing yourself and start living.

Fight your way above the many inevitable traumatizations of your ego, escape damnation by the past, and look to the opportunities of the present. I don't mean some vague moment in the present—next week or next month, perhaps. I mean today, this minute.

The past may not be your only obstacle; tomorrow-type thinking can also block you from your goals. Yearning for a new tomorrow may often be unrealistic and negative—especially if you foresee some angel coming to your rescue and pressing a magic button for you. There is no magic button—

just your own resources, your own determination, your own feeling that you have the right to succeed.

3. Stop belittling yourself. Too many people do this. Maybe you're not a celebrity or a millionaire or a football hero or an astronaut hero. You can be great if you're a sales clerk or a housewife, or a car washer or a dishwasher, or a garbage collector or a bill collector. Learn from my story about the scrubwoman with pride and courage. A scrubwoman can be a great human being.

Stop belittling yourself. If we were all movie stars, there would be no food on our tables, no production in our factories—and maybe no one to watch movies.

Accept yourself as you are. Otherwise you will never see opportunity. You will not feel free to move toward it; you will feel you are not deserving.

4. Try to set constructive goals. We have enough negativism these days, enough violence, enough cynicism.

Experiments in Australia have indicated that kangaroos do not like loud noises. Well, I'm with the kangaroos. I'm in favor of quiet, purposeful, constructive people who move toward their goals without unnecessarily loud fanfare.

I know of some people who have adopted a child; the youngster's parents died and he was needy. He needed affection; he needed a home. This couple wanted to help him, and so they adopted him. But they did it quietly. They did not boast loudly about how great they were. They just did it. I admire them as much for the way they handled themselves as I do for what they did.

I feel proud of my nephew Joe also; his goals are quietly, modestly constructive. He seeks opportunity—the opportunity to help other people lead longer, more secure lives.

I went with my wife Anne to Cambridge, Massachusetts, to see the Commencement Exercises. Our nephew was graduating from Harvard. Thousands of people had come to attend. We sat with Joe's parents in the rear, under a tree near a dirt roadway. The sun was shining and it was hot; waiting for the formal exercises to begin, I thought about my talk with my nephew the night before.

He had told me about his plans. He had been on scholarship at Harvard, in organic chemistry; now he was about to go on to his master's in biological chemistry. He told me that some research on wound healing that I published many years ago had excited him very deeply and had influenced his thinking to the point that he was determined to pursue research in chemistry, on the life of the cell. He told me of his determination to do research, to find a clue to the cure of cancer, to make a serum that would prevent it.

This was no wild-eyed boasting, no loud conceit. We discussed some technical points; we exchanged opinions. His feet were on the ground; his goal was straight ahead.

I was most pleased with his quiet purposefulness. That night I couldn't sleep. I was excited by his determination, by the wonder of his youthful belief in himself, by the thrill of the commencement exercises next day.

The commencement exercises were stormy. A student was allowed to criticize the learning process in a ten-minute lecture to the audience and following his talk one hundred students—boys and girls—walked out.

Still, the Commencement Exercises proceeded and our nephew Joe, along with many others, received his degree. An important step toward the implementation of his constructive goals.

A move toward opportunity.

5. Stand up to crises. Don't let them throw you! Fight to stay calm. As I've written in other books, even surmount the crisis completely and turn a crisis into a creative opportunity.

Refuse to renounce your self-image. No matter what happens, you must keep your good opinion of yourself. No matter what happens, you must hold your past successes in your imagination, ready for showing in the motion picture screen of your mind. No matter what happens, no matter what you lose, no matter what failures you must endure, you must keep faith in yourself. Then you can stand up to crises, with calm and courage, refusing to buckle; then you will not fall through the floor. You will be able to support yourself.

Look in the mirror. That's you. You must like yourself; you must accept yourself; you must be your own friend. In crises, especially, you must give yourself support. That is you in the mirror. Don't look at yourself narcissistically, telling yourself you're the most perfect, wonderful, godlike individual on earth, but give yourself appreciation. Remember other crises you've lived through. See in your mind the ones you handled successfully, the ones you turned into opportunities for growth. Don't let yourself down!

Opportunity and Self-Respect

Five suggestions for moving toward exciting new opportunities. I hope they help you. I think they will.

I feel that this is a key chapter in this book on self-respect because few of us are spoon-fed everything we want and need in life, and we must learn to take advantage of our constructive opportunities if we are to build good lives for ourselves—the kinds of lives that encourage us to feel a strongly embedded sense of self-respect.

In a physical sense, the American frontier and many other frontiers throughout the world are closed—but opportunities remain very much alive. And not just in Outer Space. Some of the greatest opportunities gain momentum in the Inner Space of our minds before they are ready to be propelled out into action.

In the field of education, we find people using "talking typewriters" to help children learn skills such as reading. One group of children, helped by the typewriter procedure, at the end of the first grade read at the sixth grade level—according to a prominent test.

New opportunity for children.

And adults? Plenty of opportunity for adults who go at it intelligently, rejecting the passive approach of waiting for opportunity to knock, and instead building the inner strength they need to open their eyes to opportunity, to move toward opportunity, to seize opportunity.

I mean constructive opportunity, of course, not the kind of opportunism which would enrich you while you trample all over other people en route. This kind of anti-social and inconsiderate aggression could not bolster your sense of self-respect.

Indeed, one of the great opportunities in your lifetime must be a direct attempt to build your respectful attitude toward yourself. To respect our cultural celebrities and leaders and institutions is not enough. To live well, you must respect yourself.

Living in this huge world—so heavily overpopulated that some eminent people fear the possibility of a drastic shortage of food at some future time—we are not omnipotent and must sometimes compromise or surrender.

By surrendering, we must win.

You surrender to compassion, however, not to resentment. To courage, not to cowardice.

To your assets, not to your liabilities.

And you surrender to the opportunity within you that you create for yourself—an opportunity that will lead you to richer living and greater self-respect.

Complicated person that you are, frustrated and yet confident, negative and yet positive, failure-oriented and yet success-oriented, you count down in the Inner Space of your mind, strengthen yourself and then launch yourself toward today's opportunities in your world.

CHAPTER 8

Real Forgiveness: Active Forgiveness

As a tailor giving his full attention and skill to the designing of a handsome custom-made suit, we build the full and rich power of our sense of self-respect. Each day this is our major objective; each day is D-day, and we sail forth heavily armed with weapons of peace to make new conquests—inner conquests—overcoming the shoreline to shoreline resistance of our internal negative feelings and removing from our path the mines that would detonate and destroy us. Forward we march, earning the money that gives us the realistic tools to live, and then using this precious life in a constructive way.

Ours is a very special D-day. As with the D-day of World War II in which General Eisenhower gathered together the full forces under his command and, mustering his courage and intelligence and troops, unleashed his complete concentrated drive on the enemy, we too concentrate and focus and move out. But our enemy is invisible, negative feelings; and our goal is invisible, self-respect; and our weapons are invisible (and peaceful), our ideas and feelings and images.

For us, each day is D-day and we brave the stormy seas in our fragile craft, rising above the fears of our aloneness and our mortality, rushing out of our landing craft, wave upon wave of purposeful determination, hurling ourselves upon our day's goals and grimly bayoneting the self-depreciation that would keep us from our goals.

To repeat, ours is a very special D-day. Our war is not only an invisible one, it is also a humane war, bloodless, constructive and without casualties. On our D-day—on all our D-days —we seek only our self-respect, only our status as rich human beings.

Even more, we strive to join others—of all nations and races and colors—in this battle for self-respect. On this D-day we wish self-respect for all humanity.

Furthermore, we forgive: We forgive others for their faults. We forgive others for their imperfections. We forgive others for the wrongs they have done us—and we forgive others for the wrongs which we imagine they have done us.

On this D-day—in which we cherish self-respect and forgiveness—we condemn all war. We condemn war against others, as well as war against ourselves.

For we forgive ourselves too. We forgive ourselves for all the mistakes of our lifetimes. These are many, but we forgive ourselves for them. We forgive ourselves for all our human flaws—and they are many. As Jesus Christ did, we do—we bring with us into our life forgiveness.

This is a formidable task, this nurturing of forgiveness, one of the key ingredients of self-respect—thus when we undertake to forgive every day, each day is a D-day. No half effort, no tentative stumble—a real thrust, all out, D-day.

Let us face it, the history of humanity has been a history of grudge-holding and hatred. From all the religious wars through the revolutionary wars and through our bloody twentieth-century wars, the world—as Alsace-Lorraine and Vietnam—has been a battleground in which Suspicion and Resentment and Greed have joined forces to throw and pin Forgiveness to the mat.

So on our D-day we must marshal the forces of our maturity and seasoning, to launch ourselves upon a momentous day of self-respect through forgiveness. No headlines in the newspapers, but we move forward.

What is forgiveness?

I ask this question because what we must seek is a form of forgiveness that is real.

Is forgiveness just a word? Someone wrongs you, you mumble to yourself, "I forgive him," and that's that. Is this forgiveness? Is forgiveness a magical word that you no sooner mouth than—abracadabra—you have wiped the slate clean?

Unfortunately, I do not think that forgiveness comes that easily. It seems to me that forgiveness is much more than lip service. In this sense, noting this objection, I will outline my ideas on forgiveness—which may well be different from the concept of forgiveness on which you have been reared.

To many people, forgiveness is a rather passive concept. You forgive yourself or someone else, lie down to take a catnap, and that's that. You return to the passive void and go back to half-living.

I know a very responsible middle-aged man, who is only half-alive. I meet him in the street now and then and ask, "How are you doing?"

He shrugs his shoulders, bored, and says, "I'm still alive, I get by."

Six months later, I meet him and ask, "How are you today? How do you feel?"

He shrugs his shoulders, bored, and says, "I'm still alive, I get by."

A very intelligent man, decent instincts, a good worker, a responsible family man—still, life to him is only a matter of, "I get by."

His boredom, I always feel, arises from an essentially passive way of looking at things.

To be passive is, all too often, to be half-alive.

So with forgiveness.

Passive forgiveness is not good enough. Traditional lip-service forgiveness is not good enough. For full living, we need a more active concept of forgiveness.

Real forgiveness, that which gives you a full sense of living and self-respect, is active forgiveness.

Two Stories of Forgiveness

I feel that two stories—one of passive and one of active forgiveness—will clarify my point.

First, let me tell you about husband and wife, a "forgiving" married couple.

They came to see me. They felt troubled, guilty and confused. Her mother had given them money to use to buy a house, and somehow they had lost the money. This was typical of them, I could see quickly. They lacked a sense of direction and moved toward frustration. The woman was obviously too aggressive; the man was obviously too passive.

The man had been overseas in the service. While he was away, I learned, she had been unfaithful.

Still, she apologized for what she had done and he said, "I forgive you." Surely there was hope.

Their personalities seemed to clash constantly. He worked

in the chemical industry. She was pushing him, "Why don't you ask your boss for a raise?" He was timid, and so her aggressiveness threatened him; he evaded trying to improve himself vocationally and, in an attempt to escape her domination, warned that he was intending to start flirtations with other girls.

Thus she was unsure of him, but "I would forgive him if he did," she said. "I would forgive him."

All this forgiveness, all this mouthing of the words, but what did it come to? He forgave her; she forgave him. They were still frustrated with each other in all kinds of ways and, in spite of the words they used, they seemed bent on destroying each other's self-respeect.

My feeling was that they had to learn to forgive in a real and active sense—first themselves, then each other—helping each other to fulfill themselves. She, for example, needed to curb her aggressive dominating ways and to help him to assert himself more forcefully in his work, while he needed to help her assume a more feminine role by rising to his masculine role with more assurance.

This was what they needed: real, active, functional forgiveness going beyond words to the world of goals and of meaningful activity.

Were they able to do this? I don't know. Time will tell; I am hopeful.

Now, a forgiveness success story—from a failure, an outcast, an inmate of a federal prison.

What this man had done, the nature of his crime—or crimes—I do not know, but he had been a prisoner at Leavenworth before going to the Texarkana institution in the federal prison system.

So he had much for which to forgive himself; and he did.

In an active way. He did more than mutter to himself as he moped around his chores, "I forgive myself."

At Leavenworth, struggling mightily to do something to help himself, he enrolled in a psycho-cybernetics course. Feeling himself on the road to rehabilitation, he transferred to Texarkana and got a psycho-cybernetics course started, working to rehabilitate not only himself but other inmates as well.

This is active forgiveness. He forgave himself and others. He did something about it by building his self-image, working to rechannel his life focus, accepting responsibility for himself and his actions, and by trying to help others in addition.

Quite a success story. Here was a "failure" who gave himself forgiveness, did something about it actively, started a twelve-week course to help others forgive themselves too.

This is active forgiveness.

Active Forgiveness in Action

How do you forgive so that in doing so you improve yourself as a human being and increase your sense of self-respect?

1. Use foresight. You must build your vision of a good day; this means you exercise clear thinking.

The first principle of clear thinking is to realize you are living in the present where forgiveness does not apply—for forgiveness arises out of yesterday's problems. To start forgiving, you think in terms of the here and now. Renouncing grudges, you plan your present goals, rising above the regrets of yesterday and looking forward to what the new day can bring you if you plan actively for it.

Stop looking backward to misery and mistakes; look forward to new goals and new excitement.

2. Seize opportunity. We talked about this already, and therefore I need not remind you that in seizing opportunity you do not trample on other people's toes or infringe on their rights. Opportunity-building is constructive.

When you look for opportunities and move toward opportunities, you tear yourself away from the hurts of the past. Even if these hurts remain with you somewhat, you neutralize their effect as you build your enthusiasm for new adventures. Thus you feed your soul and, satiated, you feel no need to keep piling the fires of resentment which come, to a considerable degree, from hunger and frustration.

When you reactivate your success mechanism by reaching out toward new opportunities, you drown out your frustrations with the flood of your fulfillments and with this active approach you forgive yourself and others in your generous feeling for your new living.

3. Develop your insight. Into what? Into yourself. Into other people. Into the life process itself.

As you develop insight, increasing the scope of your awareness, you build your capacity for forgiveness. Because you move out of a narrow channel of self-centeredness into a wide swath of thinking.

Understanding the imperfections of life, the imperfections of people, the limitations of circumstances, the unhappy reality of death and danger, you stop expecting perfection of yourself and of others. Thus, when you make a mistake, you can feel compassion for yourself, refusing to condemn yourself and to reduce your self-image to the size of a microbe. You can accept yourself, with insight and with the humility that insight can bring, and you can accept others too.

In developing your insight, recognize the importance of

your thinking and your imaging. Your sense of dignity is a full-time job, a lifetime accomplishment. Your capacity for forgiveness is a marvelous yardstick to measure your value as a human being. No matter what your age, you aim at daily growth and at productive involvement in your world, and at assuming responsibility for yourself and for other people.

4. Concentrate on compassion. To feel compassion—for yourself or for someone else—is a wonderful feeling. The compassionate person identifies with the problems of other people and, indeed, feels an empathy for others in their troubles. He feels for himself, too—one individual in a vast universe fighting for his place in the sun.

This is not self-pity, which is a negative attitude. It is a positive reaching out with brotherliness.

When you feel compassion, forgiveness comes easy because you understand the frailty of the human situation and the inevitability of mistakes and frustrations.

It is all right to work on your concrete goals—job, money, investments, or whatever. But break free from your more materialistic goals from time to time and concentrate on compassion, which leads to forgiveness.

5. Forget yesterday. Not completely, of course, but forget the negative quicksand in which you submerge yourself—until, in a spasm of agony, you go to your doom.

Not that your yesterdays don't have a certain importance, but, still, today is your realistic time for living—not yesterday. Too many people yearn for yesterday in a self-pitying way, yearning perhaps for days that were not nearly as wonderful as they think they were. Or they obsess themselves with the mistakes of yesterday, and the grievances of yesterday, refusing to forget them.

Forget and forgive. Or perhaps the more proper order should be forgive and then forget.

Then take an active approach to living and move forward to today's exciting goals.

6. *Try to relax.* Make this a daily goal. Because when you relax, you automatically forgive—yourself and others. You cannot relax while you're holding a grudge; when you hold a grudge, the resentment burns inside you and keeps you from relaxing.

You relax when you rise above resentment with forgiveness to pleasant thoughts and images and feel good about yourself, other people, the world you live in.

Forgiveness to relaxation to pleasure to self-respect is a fine success cycle.

Forgiveness à la Carte

This is a rather silly label for this next story, I must admit. Still, the the story did feed me—and I hope it will also nourish you.

One day I was in Philadelphia, I climbed into a cab, and the cabdriver started talking. I was trying to think about a lecture I was to make to a group of one hundred executives on the art of communication, but the cabbie was very talkative.

"You know," he started in, "the funnest thing happened to me. My wife phoned me at three o'clock in the morning."

"Does she stay out that late often?" I asked.

"Well, actually, she's not my wife anymore. I should have said, 'my ex-wife.'"

"When were you divorced?"

"Twenty years ago. And this is the first time she's called me since then."

"The first time in twenty years?"

"The first time in twenty years—when we got divorced. She woke me from a deep sleep. At first I thought maybe I was dreaming. But it was her."

"You recognized her voice?"

"Yes—after a minute."

"Why did she call you after all these years?"

"She just wanted to say hello."

"At three o'clock in the morning?"

"Right."

Hello at three o'clock in the morning after twenty years of divorce. Hello, indeed! I shoved my lecture notes back in my jacket pocket; I would talk off the cuff. Hello at three o'clock in the morning after twenty years!

"What did you say to her?"

"I said hello."

An obliging Philadelphia cabdriver—why not hello? I leaned forward in my seat. "You mean you never got in touch with her for twenty years?"

"That's right."

"What went wrong with your marriage?"

"I don't know. She was all right, I guess, but she kept telling me what to do and what not to do and what was right and what was wrong and—I tell you, she almost drove me crazy. She wanted to have her way all the time—in everything."

"And you couldn't take it?"

"That's it."

"So she got sore and left you?"

"No, buddy, *I* left. *I* left her. I was up to my ears with all her opinions. One day I couldn't stand it anymore so I bawled the hell out of her. So she says, 'If you don't like it, why don't you leave?' I didn't say a word. Why should I? She always got her way no matter what I said. I ate my dinner that night—a good meal, I remember it, she's a great cook—and I went to bed. I had a good sleep. I got up very early. She was snoring. I took a hot tub, and brushed my teeth. Then I had some cereal—and left."

"Just like that?"

"Just like that."

"No words, no fight . . .?"

"No, I had some cereal and left."

"That was twenty years ago?"

"Right."

"And you haven't seen or talked to her since?"

"Yup. Wow, wait till I tell my mother she phoned me at three in the morning!"

"Did you support her?"

"For three months. Then I disappeared. I went around the world on a boat—as a deckhand. She had the police after me, but they couldn't catch up with me."

"Where is she now?"

"Down south. She said she has a beauty parlor there."

"Did she tell you why she called?"

"She just wanted to say hello."

"Was she mad at you?"

"Nah."

"Were you mad at her?"

"Nah."

"Was she drunk?"

"She doesn't drink."

"Did she get married again?"

"Fifteen years ago, she said."

"Is she still married?"

"I don't think she is."

"Did you have any children together?"

"A boy. He was four when I left. He's twenty-four now."

"You haven't seen him since? You must miss him."

"Sure I do. But not her."

"Did she tell you what he's doing?"

"Oh, he's in the army—for good. She said he's six feet two and weighs two hundred thirty pounds." He laughed. "Can you imagine what he'd do to me if he ever got his hands on me?"

We rolled along through the streets of Philadelphia as he laughed and laughed. We passed dozens of grim, worried-looking people as we rode through the streets. The cabdriver laughed and laughed as he thought of the son he hadn't seen in twenty years.

"How old are you?" I asked him.

"Forty-seven." He was still laughing.

"Did you remarry?"

"No."

"Do you intend to marry again?"

"Not me, brother. Once is enough."

"How did you feel talking to your ex-wife?"

"It was a nice feeling. We talked about old times, and we had a lot of laughs."

"No hard feelings?"

"What for?"

"No old grudges?"

"Nah."

"Maybe she missed you."

"Maybe."

"Maybe she's sorry."

"Maybe."

"Maybe she'd like you back."

"She asked if I'd like to come down there and visit her."

"Will you?"

"No, sir."

"Why not?"

"Well, it's like this." He braked the cab and came to a stop in front of my destination. "I may not have much dough—I'm just a taxi driver—but I have one thing nobody can take away from me. And I mean nobody. That's my self-respect. She could never take that away from me. Maybe that's the only thing I do have, but do you know something, I sleep fine at night."

I got out and handed him a bill. "I've sure been talking," he said. "What about you? Are you married?"

"Yes," I said.

Then he gave me my change. "How does your wife like Philadelphia?"

"She's in New York." I tipped him.

"Oh," he said. "You left your wife, too."

"For the day only," I said. "I'm lecturing here."

"Good luck in your marriage," he said. "As for me, I'll be fine just so long as my son doesn't catch up with me." He laughed, waved, and off he went.

Forgiveness à la carte. That's what I like to call this story.

I tell you this story, because it has a certain offbeat charm, for one thing, but also because it is good medicine, I feel, for those of us who keep blaming ourselves and other people and who find it so difficult to forgive.

A marriage broken so abruptly, yet both principals gave

forgiveness to the other—in a real sense, not mouthing the words at all, but refusing to hold grudges, and going about the day-by-day job of living. Such fantastic drama—twenty years between scenes—and yet they could forgive each other without words and say hello at three in the morning.

Now, although I rather liked the cabdriver, I am definitely not holding up his actions in any positive light—for one thing, his apparent irresponsibility to his son is far from commendable. The same goes for his apparent irresponsibility toward his wife, too. Still, from all appearances, he forgave himself, his ex-wife forgave herself, each forgave the other; and, in light of their forgiveness under such drastic circumstances and the independent kind of self-respect that both people seemed to seek for themselves, perhaps the little boy had a pretty fair childhood too. I don't know, but perhaps.

I do not tell this story to praise (or to condemn) the character of either husband and wife, but primarily as a helpful aid for those who find it so hard to forgive minor mistakes. In other words, if this cabdriver could forgive himself even for these actions, why can't you forgive yourself for your small blunders?

Forgiveness and Self-Respect

Admittedly, forgiveness is no easy matter. We live in a difficult and uncertain world and, to the best of my knowledge, the world has always been difficult and uncertain.

Perhaps we can see an individual's problem in forgiving other people if we enlarge the scope of our inquiry and project it onto an international scale.

Here we see the nations of the East seething for decades in resentment at western invasions and at their repeated subjugations. We see little forgiveness or understanding on either side.

Or the blacks, murdered and enslaved many decades ago, brought from Africa and debased. Little forgiveness or understanding to this day—on either side.

Or the Irish, impoverished by Great Britain, humiliated and enraged, cornered in their arid potato farms, hungry. Decades of little forgiveness or understanding on either side.

Or Germany, never forgetting her defeat in World War I, never forgiving—until Hitler came and drove her to her doom in a spasm of maniacal resentment.

Yes, the world has seen great trouble and injustice, little understanding and formidable violence. And very little forgiveness.

Now, a person who is hounded and deprived and victimized has, in my opinion, every right to insist on fair treatment and to fight for his rights. To discriminate against anyone because of race or color or nationality, for example, is obviously an abomination—but that is not my point. My point is that nations have practiced little forgiveness through the centuries and great bodies of people have persecuted minority groups most cruelly. Seeing this unforgiveness demonstrated on a world-size scale, we can appreciate how hard it is for individual human beings, fragile human beings, to forgive each other.

When someone hurts you, do not turn the other cheek. I do not advocate turning the other cheek at all. In this and in other regards, my concept of forgiveness is active—not at all passive.

But—and here is my point—after you have actively done what you can to protect your rights and move toward your goals, at this point you would do well to see what has happened from the other fellow's point of view and try to forgive him for being human.

Maybe he didn't realize he was injuring you. Maybe he was blindly pushing forward on his goals and did not even see you in the way. Maybe he was brutal at the time but regretted this afterward. Forgive him.

Forgiveness for other people is a great achievement, the achievement of a lifetime. You rise above resentment to your real worth as a human being.

Forgive others if you can—but, more important, forgive yourself.

For this is the great forgiveness: self-forgiveness. Forgive yourself and you soar to your greatest dignity as a human being. Like Neil Armstrong, you walk on the moon. Forgive yourself and, like Galileo or Newton, you explore new areas —in yourself—areas free of guilt and taint, inner areas in which you can build yourself, a giant among men.

You can be a giant among men, because you forgive yourself; an ethical religious man, because you absolve yourself; a philosopher, because you think of your virtues; a plastic surgeon, because you remove your emotional scars; and a human being, because you thrill to the feel of life without guilt.

If you have erred, forgive yourself—not just with empty words, but actively. This is real forgiveness. Actively forgive yourself, and with your forgiveness give yourself the inner strength to move out toward your goals. Climb Mount Everest as you ask your boss for a raise you have long deserved. Fight your way through the rough waters of the English Channel as you live through a failure and, forgiving yourself, calmly eat your food and go to sleep. Hack your way through tropical jungles as you communicate, sincerely and honestly, with a fellow human being.

Real forgiveness. Active forgiveness. More than words. Forgiveness in living.

Thus each day is D-day for you, a peaceful D-day in which you plot your goals and move on them, actively forgiving yourself and others and winning your great battle for self-respect.

CHAPTER 9

The Dynamic Potential
for Mirror Watchers

THIS is an age of jets and computers, an age in which man, exploring Outer Space, has even landed and walked on the Moon. Still, we have with us in our households some of the old, familiar objects.

Like mirrors.

And we can use mirrors usefully and creatively, as a dynamic potential for our emotional growth.

Many people have said that this is an age infected with too much spectatoritis—too much watching. People render themselves too passive to life. Instead of going outside and swatting a tennis ball or belting a golf ball or swimming a few quick laps, they tend to station themselves in front of their television sets and watch someone else performing—armchair participants.

Watching. Not "doing." Just watching.

I am focusing on athletics here to illustrate my point, but I feel that we can apply this concept of too much spectator-like passivity to many areas of modern life. Too many people try, without success, to make watching substitute for doing.

You can't do it.

Because your mission in life is greater than this. You were not born into this huge, sprawling, amorphous world to passively surrender your unique God-given nature to become a depersonalized absorber of impressions, an automaton.

Try mirror watching instead.

Mirror watching can be—if exercised with an honest, creative approach—a most rewarding, enriching pursuit, in which you can combat the depersonalizing forces in our modern world and assert your individuality in a constructive sense.

The creative mirror watcher has a goal in mind; and that goal is not vanity, not narcissism, but focusing on the image within. He builds onto his self-image so that he can use this day, and the next, to move toward a more strongly entrenched feeling of self-respect.

We all know the story of Narcissus, the handsome youth who, seeing his image reflected in a pool of water, fell in love with it. According to the centuries-old legend, he was then transformed into the flower bearing his name.

We know about narcissism—or self-love—in which an individual may fixate his admiration on himself.

The creative mirror watcher, however, is not engaging in narcissism. He is not looking at himself in order to idolize his face. What he seeks is a clarification of who he is, in an emotional sense, and a sharper refocusing on the person he can become.

The man who is a creative mirror watcher, straining to make his day an exciting one, does not aim at admiring the color of his eyes or at worrying about his receding hairline; and the woman is not out to congratulate herself on her latest permanent or to criticize hastily applied powder on her cheek.

Interested in his growth as a person, the creative mirror watcher looks penetratingly for the negation of frustration or for the inner smile of confidence.

Looking at himself with kind eyes, he seeks to find in the image behind his face his sense of identity, his potential for emotional development, his capacity for self-fulfillment, his readiness to forgive himself and others and, blending all these subtle ingredients, he seeks to cook up a nourishing feeling of self-respect.

In the final analysis, this mirror watching is an exercise in orientation. What is it you see as you look at your face in the mirror? Is it not success or failure?

I have, of course, treated the success and failure mechanisms at great length in my book *Psycho-Cybernetics* (Prentice-Hall, 1960), outlining the components of these mechanisms in detail, so I will not do that here—though I will in this chapter emphasize several.

My main point is this: As you look in the mirror, searching, on one day or another, for the negative or positive forces behind your outward features, you are then placing yourself in a position to reinforce your success orientation and to fight to overcome your failure orientation.

You may make use of all your faculties and your capacity for adaptation to your environment, or you may not. The following story illustrates how important your orientation is.

The Maladjusted Pigeon

Circling my apartment in New York city is a terrace with rock gardens, trees and boxes of growing green shrubbery. Between these boxes of shrubbery are massive stone pillars, two feet square, topped by four heads of sheep; the pillars are solid stone, built in an old-fashioned way—Gothic style, perhaps—and connecting the sheep heads are *U*-shaped slabs of stone. These *U*-shaped ornaments—almost *V*-shaped, because the bottoms come to such sharp points—are a foot high and four inches wide. At the base are crevices slanting downward about three inches deep.

Many pigeons live on my terrace. Now and then, on a summer's day, while I relax on my terrace, drinking a glass or two of beer, I feed the pigeons bread crumbs.

One day a young pigeon hopped off the head of a stone sheep, where it had been perching, and wobbled toward me. It was a strange gray-white pigeon whose beak was distorted, twisted severely to the side. I threw some bread crumbs, but the only way this pigeon could pick up the food was to twist its head to the side.

It was a warm summer day—late in the afternoon—and having finished an especially hard day's work, I decided to reward myself with *two* glasses of beer. Which accounts, I guess, for the following conversation—which I relate with, of course, some artistic license:

"You see, doctor, it isn't easy for me to eat."

I nodded my head, appraising its twisted beak. "I know."

"Last time I flew down here I wanted to ask you—you're a plastic surgeon—can't you fix my beak?"

"It's not easy," I said.

"I see. You don't want to do it because I haven't any money."

"No, that's not it."

"Then why don't you give me a break?"

It was a lazy, hazy summer afternoon. Below, people were surging from the skyscraper office buildings, milling underground in the hot subways, homeward-bound. Above, were sunshine, sky and clouds—yellow, blue and white—with little birds and huge jets whirling through the skies. Reality and unreality, meeting and separating.

"Okay," I said. The pigeon seemed a nice little fellow. "We'll admit you to the hospital later. We'll give you a checkup and if your blood pressure is normal, we'll go ahead and operate."

"Thanks, doc. You don't know what it will mean to me— eating like every normal pigeon."

Then this small, twisted pigeon—"The Runt"—flew off, fluttering its wings to say goodbye, then soaring higher and higher and gone.

I noticed Brownie then—a pigeon I had nicknamed Brownie—this pigeon had visited me dozens of times.

Brownie, with a swishing of wings, whirled from atop a box of shrubbery to take up position on a *U*-shaped crevice between the heads of two stone sheep. It was only four inches wide.

How could she balance herself in such a narrow crevice? I did not know how, but she did it.

Facing south, she balanced herself on her left clawed foot, hiding the other in her feathers. Aside from moving her wings now and then to keep her balance, she remained immobile in this absurd position for close to an hour.

I was fascinated by the awkwardness of her posture, and by the stubbornness with which she maintained it. I glanced at my watch—time for dinner soon—but still Brownie continued to face south, balanced in her narrow *U*-shaped crevice on her left foot, the other foot concealed beneath her feathers.

Then, by some miracle, she managed to turn around in her constricted resting-place. Now she was facing north, balanced on her right foot. Five minutes passed, but she stayed in her new, equally uncomfortable position, seeming to remain unruffled in spite of making the worst of all possible adjustments to the possibilities in her pigeon world.

I had to talk to her about this—again, exercising my imagination just a little:

"Hello, Brownie," I said.

"Hello."

"What are you doing there?"

"I live here."

"You mean you sleep there?"

"Of course. Where have you been?"

"All the time?"

"Sure. For months."

"But you must be uncomfortable. You must feel cramped. You are off balance."

"It is my home."

"But there are so many nicer places on my terrace."

"I'm used to this place."

"Brownie, now let's be reasonable." I leaned forward in my chair. "Why stand on one foot facing the wrong direction when you can stand, comfortably, on one of my shrubbery boxes on both feet, facing the right direction?"

"But I'm used to this."

I must make a confession: occasionally I lose my temper, and I lost it now. What triggered it was the sight of this pigeon—still awkwardly balanced on one foot, twisted to face the wrong direction in terms of the configuration of its body, unmoving. "Look," I shouted. "I just want to help you. You can't feel happy in such an uncomfortable position. It's impossible."

"But I'm used to it." Pointing her nose upward, pigeon

style, she indicated her annoyance with my attempts to make her change.

My conversations with pigeons were over for the day. It was almost seven o'clock. New York's office buildings were now strangely deserted, but people, in lesser numbers, walked the streets below. Above, the sun was cooling and, on my rock-gardened terrace, with the massive stone pillars, one small pigeon, body twisted, clung stubbornly to her adopted home.

I went in to dinner.

Which Way Are You Facing?

Look in the mirror to focus more clearly on your orientation. Which way are you facing? Are you headed toward success, or toward failure?

Too many people live one-dimensional lives, tragically clinging. With pigeon-minded persistence, they refuse to change even when they can improve the quality of their living through doing so.

Too many people—like Brownie the pigeon—use only one leg when they have two legs, in the sense that, fearfully, they lead over-limited lives, refusing, because of their sense of inferiority, to step out strongly into the world on two firm legs that give them genuine movement and mobility.

Too many people—like Brownie the pigeon—fail to see possibilities for improvement and, emotionally distorted, lack perspective.

To repeat. Which way are you facing? Ask yourself this, mirror watchers, as you look for the image behind your physical image—your self-image.

Do you insist on holding fast to a dull non-living existence because of past guilts, mistakes, or fears?

Mired deep in a sense of your inadequacy, do you move about on one leg instead of two, unable to capitalize on your resources?

Do you, clinging to false beliefs about yourself, encase yourself in a tiny niche, limping through life with complaints and worries, telling yourself that's all you can make out of life?

Do you paralyze your sense of adventure with stand-pat cliches, adapting yourself listlessly to small-mindedness and a merry-go-round without music that goes around in circles of inertia?

Pigeon-headed, like Brownie, do you tell yourself that life is boring and that there is no better outlook for you and that you're "used to" things as they are?

Standing at poolside looking down into the glistening blue waters, cool and refreshing, do you refuse to take the plunge?

In short, mirror watchers, do you orient yourself toward failure as a way of life, "pigeonholing" all your worthwhile goals until mañana?

If so, communicate this to yourself as you look at yourself in the mirror—your mirror for finding truth. Communicate this to yourself and set about changing your orientation.

Stop facing toward failure!

Resolve to change direction and face toward success!

It may not be easy, but this must be your goal: to use both legs, both arms, all your resources—emotional and physical—to drive you toward success, on all cylinders.

Move toward success, in many-faceted terms. Look, not just for financial success, but for success as a human being who can give to other people, as a human being who can be a brother, as a human being who feels respect for what he is and for what he can become.

Are you willing to make the effort to find the uniqueness within you, the potency, the self-respect?

Or are you willing to settle for a life of dullness and changelessness, living in a narrow space, on one leg, constricted, your potential crushed?

The other pigeon in my little story, who I called "The Runt", tried (with a little imaginative help) to improve herself, tried to get help to overcome her handicap.

You must do this constantly: Work to overcome your handicaps, whatever they may be.

This is real movement toward self-respect.

Stop Cooking Up Failure!

In *Macbeth*, surely a masterpiece of mood, Shakespeare uses the three witches to build a feeling. They circle malevolently, cooking up a premonition of evil fully as noxious as the nauseating ingredients which they put in the pot. You sit in the audience watching the witches and—even if you never saw *Macbeth* before or read it—you cannot escape the sense of evil that they convey.

This is one of the basic functions of mirror watching: To intercept not evil, but failure. To catch impending signs of failure before they develop. To see failure in the making, head it off, and reorient yourself toward success.

Let me tell you another story:

A man came to see me. He had read *Psycho-Cybernetics*. He was forty years old and very unhappy. He had been an only child in a troubled family. Other professional help had failed to change him.

"I lost my job," he said, "two months ago. I was selling insurance, but I wasn't selling enough. I really prefer the investment business, anyway. I was glad to get rid of this job."

"How do you feel about your chances now?" I asked.

"Now?"

"Yes, now."

"Well," he said, "you write about having a goal, a worthwhile goal that is right for you. I think of good ideas and I want to follow through but then the same thing always happens. Always."

"What?"

"I can't control the negative thoughts that hit me—I feel that I'm no good, that I'm a failure, that I'll lose. These negative thoughts—I don't know what's the matter with me. I end up getting drunk, and I get fat from overeating."

I could see he was overweight, though not drastically so. But, drastically, he was overloaded with depression and failure and self-defeating drives. Here he was truly overweight.

"The other day," he said, "I was driving in Boston. I was thinking what a failure I am. I tried to resolve to diet and think thin. But then I started thinking of this pizza place in the suburbs. I tried to shake this thought, I was trying to lose weight—but I couldn't shake it. Well, you know—pizza, beer. Some diet."

His background had been troubled, and he described it despairingly—masochistic mother, alcoholic father, alcoholic uncle, alcoholic grandmother and grandfather.

"I never felt loved," he said. "I'd like to love somebody. Maybe I don't know what I feel—anyway, I get drunk maybe three times a week."

"Your mother didn't drink?"

"No, she never drank. She had a sense of shame and guilt

for the whole family. She hated herself, and hated that I had to grow up with all the drinking going on."

"She wanted you to grow up with self-respect?"

"I guess."

"But you haven't?"

"No. I try, but I fail at everything."

"Did you ever have a good girl friend?"

"Who would want me?"

"Girls could like you . . ."

"Oh, come on."

". . . if you liked yourself."

"I try."

"How?"

"I do what you say. I try to relax—I close my eyes—and I try to picture myself happy."

"And then?"

"Nothing happens," he said. "But nothing. All I get is lots of thoughts about what a failure I am. And let's be frank about it—I'm not much good."

"Is there anything you want to accomplish?"

"Sure."

"What's that?"

He leaned forward. "I want to feel good," he snapped.

"And what else?"

A spark in his eyes; for the first time, I saw determination. "I want to have good thoughts. I want to make money. I want a good emotional life."

"Anything else?"

Lightning sizzling from the heavens, the words bolted from him. "I don't want to be poor anymore. I've been poor since I was a kid. I don't want to be alone. I want friends. I want leisure. I want a good life."

Ah, I thought, here, in this passion for life, here was the

hope for him. Aloud, I said, "You must feel better about yourself."

His shoulders slumped, and he fell back, dejected once more, into his chair. "That's not easy."

"That's true," I said. "It's not easy. It's not easy at all. You've had some rough experiences. Rising above them is not easy. But what you have to feel is this: It is possible.

"Every day you must work to improve your opinion of yourself. You must forgive yourself for your failures and forget them; you must forgive your mother, too. You are not responsible for your family problems; you did not create them. You must have compassion for yourself, for your past troubles and problems—but you must not drown in them. You are more than troubles and problems and failures. You are a human being—you fight, you try, just now I saw you fighting, in your eyes I saw you fighting for your right to lead a good life, and I heard you, too. You have a right to feel happy and successful—if you work for it. You have a right to block off negative feelings and give yourself peace of mind. Do you want to exercise these rights?"

He nodded his head.

"Every day, make it a goal to try to feel better about yourself. Forget the past. Concentrate on the present. Live today.

"Every day look at yourself in a mirror: You have two images you can see—the unloved, deprived, frustrated person from an alcoholic home or the confident, successful person you can be."

"I have no successes to see."

"Yes, you have. They may be few—but you have successes—and if you can regain your successful feeling, your successful image of yourself, if you can bring it full-strength into your imagination, if you can keep this good feeling about yourself alive in your imagination, then when you look in the mirror you will see there possibilities for moving toward success."

He shook his head. "I can't remember any successes. I get drunk and I eat too much. I'm overweight. I can't hold a job. I haven't even got a girl. Why, I. . . ."

"All right," I said. "You've had more than your share of failures. But you have had that success feeling. Maybe not often—but a few times, anyway, and that's all you need. I know you've had it. I saw it. Just a few minutes ago. Your eyes flashed with determination—I saw you—and you talked like a man who had a goal, many goals, that he believed in. You talked passionately about them, without guilt or fear— for a few seconds—and that was a success."

"It was?" he said.

"Yes," I said, "that was one of your moments of success. Forget your failures; remember that moment."

Shortly he left, but he came to see me four months later. He was still depressed. He was trying hard, but he could not feel good about himself. I told him to keep trying.

A year later, he came to see me. He had lost twenty pounds and was in the investment business. He felt better about himself at times, though at other times he still hated and despised himself. He was trying hard to live in the present; time would tell whether or not he would make it. We shook hands, and I told him to keep trying.

Mirror Watching and Your Potential

We live in a world of positives and negatives—and we ourselves, citizens of this world, are composites of positives and negatives.

Injustice in this world? Yes. I never bury my head in the sand to deny it.

Humanity, by and large, has historically lived through centuries of enslavement. Until the Industrial Revolution, the common man labored from dawn till dusk. Until the Reformation, the common man had no freedom to think about religion.

In India, grave injustices have for centuries been inflicted upon groups of people called "untouchables." These poor people have for centuries been chained to an inferior status because of some supposed wrong committed in a previous life. Brutally unjust—yet reality for many, many years.

In our nation, today, we have great privilege—but injustice, too.

Still, the greatest injustices today, by and large, are the injustices you inflict on yourself:

When you consign yourself to failure.

When you refuse to forgive yourself for past mistakes.

When you deny yourself the right to happiness.

There is a scientific experiment that was performed on frogs. Live frogs were placed into tubs of water and slowly, ever so slowly, the water was heated. The question was this: When would the frogs, feeling the danger of ever-mounting heat, become alarmed and leap out of the tub to save their lives? Slowly, more heat. Slowly. Ever so slowly. More heat. Still more heat. But applied so slowly, so imperceptibly, the frogs did not notice it. Without even attempting to escape, the frogs boiled to death.

Which brings me back to Brownie the pigeon, who had grown accustomed to her uncomfortable perch on my terrace. These frogs were "used to" what seemed to them the same temperature of water—so slowly was the heat applied.

In accepting uncritically what they were used to, the pigeon endured endless discomfort and the frogs met their horrible fate.

And my point is this: You must not accept a life in which —because you are habituated to it or because you are afraid of change—you bore yourself to death.

You must not short-change yourself, denying yourself the right to live fully, insensitive to the possibilities of more successful adaptations to a world in which you must create your own justice for yourself.

Every day, be a creative mirror watcher, looking for success, not failure, out to find your dynamic potential—even if you are over sixty-five, like me. At least, I think I am over sixty-five—I don't really waste my time counting, I just love to use my time living.

Look in the mirror for the image behind your physical image.

Don't be afraid! That face won't bite you. It's you—and you must give yourself justice. You must be your best friend.

You've seen that face before? You're tired of looking at the same nose, the same eyes?

Oh, but you're not looking at nose or eyes. You're looking behind them into your self-image.

A creative mirror watcher, you look through failure to success. You look through obstacles to goals. You look through mistakes to accomplishments. You look through a sense of inferiority to a sense of self.

A creative mirror watcher, you seek to unearth your full potential as a human being.

Doing the best job with yourself that you possibly can, congratulating yourself for your determination to better yourself, you move toward a feeling of self-respect that gives sunshine to your days.

CHAPTER 10

Tear Down Those Prison Walls!

On we go in our great treasure hunt, searching for our self-respect.

Ours is a hunt which requires effort, application, and determination—not a children's game, in which we scamper around digging up objects superficially hidden here and there.

To locate our treasure—our self-respect—we must gather all the energies we possess so that we can overcome the defeatism of negative feelings, preoccupation with meaningless superficialities, and our empty, non-living tendencies.

How do we do this?

Explaining this, plotting the route, is the purpose of this book. Summarizing our progress to this point, we place stress on developing our understanding—of ourselves and of others—and on building an attitude of sincerity, carried forward into the world. We, in addition, stand guard vigilantly, sentries always alert, protecting ourselves against the internal undermining triumvirate of deadly enemies: uncertainty, resentment, and emptiness. We will refuse to compromise with this trio—we will not let them take hold of us.

What then?

We look for opportunity. We do not wait for it to knock; no, sir, we actively seek it. We will look for opportunity on worthwhile routes toward objectives which will enrich us, aiming to build our success feeling without hurting or trampling on our fellow brothers and sisters of the human race.

We forgive ourselves and others—actively, not passively. We rise above lip service, to ideals of forgiveness that float meaninglessly heavenward, to a sense of forgiveness that is active, concrete, visible and human.

Our tools are thoughts and images, success-feelings and goals—they are very powerful tools. We can use them in many creative and individual ways—as in mirror watching, when we look in the mirror to discover or rediscover the good in ourselves, the success in ourselves, the meaning for our lives.

Now, let us tear down those prison walls!

Prison walls?

Yes, now let us tear down the prison walls that you have built around yourself, walls inside which you serve your life sentence, stone which blocks your emotional movement, confines you rigidly so that you live your days passive and bored, and isolates you from other people until, in solitary confinement, your soul dies while your body lives on.

A drastic statement?

Maybe so, but I do not doubt that millions and millions spend their lives, eating themselves up with guilt and shame, punishing themselves for their past mistakes or even their very human feelings, submerging themselves in a beehive imprisonment in which they sting and sting themselves as a way of life. They have political freedom, but they are not free; they have life and breath, but are not really alive; and they have mobility, but are emotionally immobilized.

Our convict population consists of human beings waiting inside prison walls, dreaming of freedom.

Millions of other people—who are free to walk the streets, the parks, and the beaches, free to work in offices, factories, and on farms—build walls around themselves. They sabotage their own positively channeled aggression and, in deformed and excessive conformity, they crush their best human feelings. Even worse, they are "stool pigeons" who inform on themselves; they accuse themselves of crimes; and they condemn themselves to their bleak internal prisons.

The aim of this chapter is liberation from self-imposed imprisonment.

Handling Tragedy and Disillusionment

First, why do people build walls around themselves? Why do they restrict and confine themselves—unnecessarily straitjacketing their emotions and handcuffing their natural aggressiveness?

There are, of course, many reasons; complexity is, unfortunately, often the rule in life. But I think it is likely that many people imprison themselves in shocked reaction to terrible tragedy or disillusionment.

Someone beloved has died or suffered a grievous misfortune—or some close friend or member of the family has given them (or so they think) an unforgivable blow, depriving, deserting, rejecting. Worse still, many people feel responsible for a catastrophe that happened to someone else.

Recoiling in horror from life's uncertainties and dangers, fleeing from difficult reality, they then may build prison walls around themselves in frightened defensiveness, resigned to spending their lives imprisoned, bored, not really living— but *safe.*

Now we must face this: Our lives are not Cinderella stories—there is no magic coach with horses and no one waving a wand over our destinies. Most of us will have to cope with tragedy and disillusionment at least a few times in our lives; so we'd better learn to deal with it.

A loved one may die—that is reality. We may suffer loss of job, or money, or status, or our business may collapse— that is reality. We may be rejected: by a friend, a sweetheart, our wife or husband, our mother or our father—that, too, is reality.

How do we deal with tragedy and disillusionment? How do we handle despair and grief? How do we live with the disappointed awareness that sometimes we are powerless to control crucial forces in our lives?

We feel sorrow—we are human beings, and it is as simple as that. We feel sorrow, we feel deprivation, we feel resentment. We are not made of stone, so we react. Unashamedly, we may feel depressed; without guilt, we may feel discouraged. It may take us time to rally our fighting spirit and get back to ourselves, but we will.

We must get back to ourselves—this is the key to handling crushing tragedy or disillusionment. We must fight our way through our depression, our sadness and our rage and get back to our successful way of seeing life, and of seeing ourselves. It may take time, but we must rally our feelings of enthusiasm and adventure and begin living fully again.

The alternative is building stout defenses to protect us— prison walls.

It may be that you have imprisoned yourself emotionally

without experiencing the trauma of tragedy or disillusionment. In any case, my basic point is this: If you have built prison walls around yourself, you are only half alive. You owe yourself more than that. You must tear them down if you want to live fully. There is no other way. Money cannot do it for you, and neither can property or material goods or travel or anything else.

Only you can do it.

Prisoner, tear down those prison walls!

The Bus Driver and the Salesman

Let me tell you two more stories—one about a bus driver and one about a salesman.

The bus driver was in his early thirties. He was a slim, good-looking, young fellow, but I noted a listless and unhappy look in his eyes. He came to see me; and we had a long talk.

"You have to help me," he said. "I feel rejected. Maybe I'm not much, I don't know. I feel filled with rejection. Every time I meet a girl, she rejects me. They all do."

We saw things through different eyes, he and I. I saw a slim, clean-cut, good-looking young fellow—he saw only "rejection." I asked him about himself.

"Girls turn me down," he said. "All the time. They don't like me."

"You're a good-looking guy," I said.

"They reject me. Well, not completely. Twice I almost got married, but they were pushing me so hard for marriage that I rejected them."

"You rejected them?"

"Yeah, come to think of it, I did."

"Tell me about yourself. About your family."

"My father's dead, he died when I was twelve. He was a good father, I guess, but he smacked me around, I really didn't like him much. I liked my mother better—she was kind of bossy, though. Anyway, sometimes I used to wish my father was dead. When he died, I think I felt responsible."

"What did he die of?"

"He had a heart attack."

"And why did you feel you were responsible?"

"Well, I remember I wished he was dead. More than once I wished that. Then he died."

"Did you kill him, or did he have a heart attack?"

"He had a heart attack—of course."

"Then it's ridiculous to think you were responsible for his death. Don't you realize that?"

"Yes, but. . . ."

"You must stop blaming yourself for your thoughts. He used to hit you, and sometimes you hated him—but you are not responsible for his death. He had a heart attack."

We talked about his current life. He was a bus driver, lived with his mother, and rejected himself constantly. As he talked, I could see the walls of inhibition and of limitation he had built around himself—perhaps in reaction to his father's sudden death when he was twelve. (I couldn't really be sure of this.) He thought of himself as a prisoner; he had even built his own prison.

"As far as I can tell," I said, "you are living in the past. You keep rejecting yourself—maybe it's because you still blame yourself for your father's death. But remember this: You are thirty-one now, not twelve. Your father has been dead nineteen years. You must stop blaming yourself for whatever happened in the past—especially since you didn't even do anything. It was a tragedy for you that your father died when you were twelve, but you've got to stop hating yourself and live in the present. Today. Accept yourself. Look at yourself kindly. Forget the girls who have rejected you. Forget the girls who you have rejected. Live today."

Now the salesman.

I met him in Memphis, Tennessee, where I was speaking to a thousand or so salesmen on the art of communicating to other people through your own self-respect.

I was on the speaking platform early and watched the people crowding into the auditorium. It was hot. People came in, took their seats, then removed their suit jackets.

A man in a light summer suit walked down the aisle—he was gray-haired, slim, in his fifties. He caught my attention as he moved halfway down the aisle—because I could not see his hands.

I watched him as he worked his way past other people and took a seat at the side. Laboriously, he removed his suit coat. In his shirtsleeves now, he sat down again.

Now it was clear; he had no hands.

It didn't seem to bother him at all. Two other men came over to join him and they chatted companionably until I began my lecture.

He listened attentively as I talked. I was fascinated by him because he seemed so contented in spite of his handicap, and I found myself frequently facing in his direction.

Later, I talked to him. He told me about himself, and I felt extremely moved. About eleven or twelve years before, he had been crippled in a railroad accident.

Before the accident, he was physically sound. Afterwards, he had no hands. For a while he thought of suicide. Finally he rejected this idea, but what next for him?

A few years passed, and then he read my book *Psycho-Cybernetics*, which, he told me, gave him new hope.

He had a goal in mind—selling machinery parts for a local concern. He moved relentlessly toward his goal. He began thinking once again in terms of success; he began setting in motion his old success images. He was selling; he was selling well. Now—with no hands—he was a top-flight salesman.

He talked with me a while, then turned to greet someone else he knew. A friend of his came over to talk to me about him. "He's not this way all the time," he said. "He has artificial hands. Why he even drives his own car."

The "handicapped" man turned around, a smile on his face. "Too damned hot," he said. "I didn't feel like wearing them."

Without a trace of embarrassment, he laughed. His friends laughed, too—without self-consciousness. No need for self-consciousness, or pity, or tact.

This handicapped man had no handicaps. For a few years after the accident he had lived in his own prison, yes. But, now, the walls were gone. He had no hands, but he could laugh—and he was free.

He had brightened my day for me.

Unlocking Your True Personality

Now, how about brightening your own day?

How?—by tearing down those prison walls, and unlocking your true personality.

Here is the crux of the problem. If, in fear, you have built prison walls around yourself, defending yourself against your feelings and against your basic humanity, you are only half alive. Your true personality is imprisoned—you might not even be aware it exists. Don't you want to get in touch with yourself as you really are, hiding behind those stout walls?

Here are my ideas on how you readjust yourself if you wish to try to liberate yourself from your self-imposed jail:

1. Get in contact with your aggressiveness. Understand that you have the right to be aggressive if you don't use aggressiveness to hurt and destroy other people. Misdirected aggressiveness is oriented toward failure, but constructive aggressiveness is essential if you are to express yourself fully, build your sense of self, and move toward your goals. If you have denied yourself the right to exercise constructive aggressiveness, you must unchain yourself from this prohibition.

2. Focus on your goals. You are ready to do this when you have given yourself the right to aggressiveness. Indeed, aggressiveness needs goals just as goals need aggressiveness.

Each day have a goal, or goals. Ask yourself where you're going and what you want to accomplish. Don't accept inertia and aimlessness. It's great to be alive, it really is. You can move in all kinds of exciting directions—life is full of rich possibilities.

Sometimes you'll be frustrated, sure. Sometimes you will, defeat yourself, or others will, or external forces beyond your control will defeat you.

But, then, there's always another day—and new goals. Goals that mean something to you. Not to others, to you.

Set your goals. Then feel that aggressive spirit and channel it so that you move toward the realization of your goals. Toward success. Out of prison, and moving forward. Concretizing the fresh feel of your real personality, free to seek constructive self-expression.

3. Accept your individuality. Understand that you don't have to be just like everyone else; you have a right to differ from other people.

In *The Magic Power of Self-Image Psychology* (Prentice-Hall, 1964), I wrote at length about the problems of conformity in our increasingly mechanized and standardized civilization. This is still a difficult problem for many people, who may inhibit themselves drastically and needlessly, imprisoning their true personalities, so they can act the way they think other people expect them to act.

Now, civilized men pay a price for the safeguards and the rewards of civilization; they must follow a number of rules for the good of all. When you're driving a car, for example, you stop when the light turns red. This is a rule—and there are others—to which you must conform.

But you have a right also to preserve the uniqueness of your personality; you have a right also to insist on your individuality. When you place yourself emotionally behind prison walls, locked up behind bars, you overconform. In an emotional sense, you wear the same uniform as everyone else and live cooped up in a tiny cell; you cannot let yourself expand when the opportunity arises.

It is basic to my theory of Psycho-Cybernetics that you live in your own image—not as someone else would like to see you. This is liberating; you create and build.

If you have locked up your real personality, hiding it from a world you fear, fight for the courage to unlock it—to give it freer and more constructive expression. Then build on your new, success-oriented, goal-bound, self-created personality and feel the self-respect grow.

The Woman Who Couldn't Talk

"Okay," you may think, "I'm more inhibited than I need to be. I never assert my opinion—not even with friends. But these prison walls you write about, I just can't tear them down."

Why not?

"Because I'm used to them, I guess."

Lo and behold! We are back in the last chapter with our stubbornly misoriented pigeon—facing in the wrong direction, awkward, but unable to change. This is the power of habit, the tyrannical power of habit.

Change is no easy process. Our habits help us to function without thinking; changing basic habits may be painful.

Even with young children, who must change their habit patterns in order to grow up, we see the slowness of change often. A very young child may throw a ball and forget it. It may take many, many months before he thinks to observe the trajectory of the ball in the air.

With adults, habits are deeply embedded. Change can be most difficult.

But impossible?

Not at all.

Let me tell you, for example, about the woman who couldn't talk.

There was no organic problem. She *could* talk; but she didn't, because she was terribly shy and dreaded talking to people.

I met her after a lecture I delivered. She came up to me and started telling me about herself: How shy she had been! How, although a woman, she almost felt like standing up when other people came into a room where she was sitting!

How lonesome she felt! She was married, had two children —but she often wondered why had her husband married her. At many social occasions she couldn't talk to anyone, so great was her feeling of inferiority.

Most gratifyingly, she told me that she had begun to change, to talk, to break out of her unreasonable prison walls two years before after reading my book *Psycho-Cybernetics*.

She set a goal for herself: a job in real estate, selling houses. This goal fired her with enthusiasm. She got her job, and she worked at it. She began to find her proper image and to lose her shyness. To sell, she had to talk and she did talk. She talked enough to sell homes to people, and more people. She talked with enough enthusiasm to become one of the top real-estate salesmen in the area.

Talkative, friendly, she told me of how once she just couldn't get herself to talk.

In two years, she had changed. She had broken through her self-imposed imprisonment to real achievement and self-respect. This woman forgot her awkwardness and self-consciousness while involved in the dynamic process of doing. Out in the world, doing, concentrating on her goals, feeling her love for life, she used a practical activity as a fulcrum through which she climbed to a new sense of confidence.

This points to one of the key concepts of psycho-cybernetics: that you use your imagination to build your success feelings and formulate goals, and then take action in constructive ways.

You all have interests—and they may lead you, too, along the road to creativity and productive self-realization.

When you express yourself through them—positively, purposefully, assertively, and bubbling with life—you are tearing down those prison walls.

Thanksgiving Every Day

Do you remember, when you were a youngster, reading about the first Thanksgiving?

Our ancestors in New England decided to set a date for giving thanks for the year's harvest. It was a rather disappointing harvest that year—1621—but they were grateful for it. Feeling a spirit of generosity, they also sent an invitation to the nearby Indians; Chief Massasoit and his followers accepted and dispatched their contribution to the feast: five robust deer. The joyous feeling of reaching out in friendship was contagious; the Plymouth Colony sent out a hunting party to shoot wild turkey and other game and they returned from the wilds with game aplenty. At home, the women were busy making corn bread and preparing cranberries. At our first Thanksgiving the tables were piled high.

Huge fires blazed outdoors; turkey, deer and other delicious meat sizzled as the New Englanders and the Indians, in friendship, enjoyed the first Thanksgiving feast in our national history.

It lasted three days. There was feasting, singing and dancing and wrestling and running races and even a cannon salute. Everybody gave thanks—for the food, the warm fires, and the joy of being alive in an era when people lived short lives and had to take full advantage of their opportunities for celebration.

You, too, give thanks that you are alive. Make the most of every day.

We are, I fear, living in an age of pessimism. Too often, we overlook our blessings and obsess ourselves with our anxieties.

Unlock your real, basic personality. Seek your real wealth

—your creative self-expression, your freedom to accept yourself as a dynamic and unique individual, and your ability to see yourself as a person of importance who has the right to happiness.

To stop the flow of your happiness is easy. You can always find a newspaper headline to frighten you or a negative-thinking acquaintance to depress you. You can always find a disease to worry about—or economic pressures, or taxes, or other images of some vague impending catastrophe. You can always feel rejected when others frown instead of smiling at you.

But you are the provider of your happiness. You are the host at your feast of Thanksgiving. You are the one who must stoke high your blazing fires of contentment.

You, with your good opinion of yourself, through the good graces of your self-image, can pile your tables high with the emotional food that can sustain you through good days and bad—until you reach out to the Thanksgiving feast that is success.

Even when your harvest is disappointing—when your income falls, or your marriage is at low tide, or you have a fight with your boss, or your car needs overhauling and you don't have the money—if, in your imagination you feast on vibrant images of your past successes, you can heal your wounds, feel the strength of your resources and give thanks. You can even, exulting in your resurgent strength, extend the hand of generosity to other people, giving them your spirit of Thanksgiving and of self-accepting plenty.

Thanksgiving can come every day in which, unafraid of the unknown terrors of inner space, you tear down those prison walls that block your constructive, goal-directed aggressiveness and keep your self-image weak.

Thanksgiving can come every day in which, freeing yourself from unrealistically constricting inhibitions, you live for that day (for your new creative day), feasting on the joys of what the new day will bring you.

Thanksgiving can come every day in which, rising above your past failures and forgiving yourself for all your mistakes and human imperfections, you choose to warm yourself with images of success and feast anew on what you can make of the new day.

And, most important, Thanksgiving can be celebrated even on a bad day, a wretched day, a day in which everything goes wrong, a day in which you move from mistake to mistake. Even on such days you can still accept yourself, still you support yourself, still you feed yourself.

But, first, you must tear down those prison walls and, unchaining your inner resources, find yourself and develop yourself as the kind of person you want to be.

This is no easy task. It takes hard work, and it takes patience and determination.

Moreover, the freedom you seek is a responsible form of freedom. In terms of your actions, you must of course follow some rules and obey our laws. I advocate freeing your personality of unreasonable limitations, not irresponsibility. When you escape from your emotional imprisonment, you don't go around stepping on other people's toes; you use your new, hard-won freedom constructively.

And then?

Self-respect.

You must respect yourself because you are trying, oh so earnestly, to find yourself as a free person.

You must respect yourself because your aims are constructive, and you seek to give—to yourself and to other people.

You must respect yourself because your goal is so worthwhile, and because it is necessary to achieve your greatest possible fulfillment as a human being.

CHAPTER 11

Tranquillity and Self-Respect

NEXT stop in our voyage of exploration is: tranquillity. Tranquillity with two *l*'s instead of one because we need it so much.

Into the second half of the twentieth century we go, where the great masses of struggling humanity search—for food to eat, clothes to wear and money to give them security. Rising above these basic considerations, they search for their identity as creative, well-motivated, integrated people—no easy task in an overpopulated, changing world in which an individual may feel like a meaningless speck in an endless universe.

This search for the best that is in us is our search for self-respect—with tranquillity.

My *Webster's Dictionary* allows this word to be spelled with either one or two *l*'s; but, to repeat, I spell "tranquillity" with two *l*'s, to get the most out of it.

When you go to buy a suit, you try it on first to see if it fits. The shoulders, the waist, the back of the suit jacket, do they fit? The trousers? How about the waist and the length? Do they fit? No matter how exquisite the suit, it will not look good on you if it doesn't fit.

The same principle applies to self-respect; a turbulent, volatile self-respect will not wear well. It will not give you satisfaction. The suit of self-respect you wear each day must come from stronger material; look for one-hundred percent tranquillity on the label.

Tranquillity is next in our voyage in search of self-respect. We must not bypass this stop; for if we do, we may destroy the meaning of the whole voyage.

Recently we were, via television, witnesses to one of the great exploratory voyages in the history of the human race: landing a man on the moon. Who would have believed it? When I was a kid, we talked about moon travel as something silly and impossible—like Santa Claus or "haunted houses." Who would have believed it: a man on the moon?

Yet, there they were, our three astronauts, on their way to the moon. With our own eyes, we saw them reach the moon. We saw it on television; when I was a kid, we didn't even have television.

There was Neil Armstrong, the first human being to set foot on the moon in the history of the world. Deftly, they avoided a crater, and there they were on the surface of the moon in their lunar module. Armstrong walked on the moon. Then Buzz Aldrin walked on the moon. The two men walked on a Sea of Tranquillity; they walked on the solid surface, weighing only one sixth of their weight on earth, and their small footprints carved out a "giant leap" for the entire human race.

What did they find? Superficially, they found rocks, dust, craters, a barren wasteland with no sign of life. Further findings? Time will tell.

Thousands and thousands of people, and thousands more, were involved in this great adventure of mankind—and billions and billions of dollars financed it. Man on the moon. What a magnificent adventure; what can approach it in excitement?

There is just one adventure—a personal adventure—one for which you do not need billions of dollars or the teamwork of thousands upon thousands of helpers. This great voyage is particularly remarkable in that transportation is free.

Your destination? The land of tranquillity.

Others have made it before you—but it is a crucial voyage for you to take in your determined search for self-respect. You may not make headlines with your spectacular technical virtuosity. Your tools are not even visible. But *you* will understand the importance of your accomplishment.

A momentous success in Outer Space, wonderful! A soul-building exercise in Inner Space, more power to you!

There are millions of anguished, suffering people in our world, forever running, jumping hurdles, vaulting over obstacles, tripping themselves up, tying themselves in knots, and rushing—forever rushing.

Your destination is more promising. The land of tranquillity has no rocks or craters and no dusty, barren wasteland without life. You will find greenery all around you, refreshing and stimulating; gorgeous flowers of all colors scent the air lovely with their perfume; luscious fruits grow on strong trees; and nourishing vegetables can be found in abundance. Is this what the land of tranquillity looks like? Or is this fantasy?

You tell me; because you create this land. As the director of your destiny, as the governor of your personality, as the commander of your forces, you create this land of tranquillity inside yourself.

How?

That is what we will consider in this chapter—the creation of tranquillity leading to self-respect. The heart of your search for the good life.

A voyage of exploration, in the most genuine sense. Don't wait for tomorrow; start today.

Your Daily Dozen for Tranquillity

Now, in reverse, I will briefly spell out your daily dozen for tranquillity: twelve negative forces that you must combat if you are to succeed in reaching the land of tranquillity. Afterward, I will spell it out in greater detail.

Every day, in your mind, while you are taking a walk or quietly sitting in a chair, when you have time, focus on these twelve negative forces and wage war on them—so that you can have peace.

Tranquillity, how to lose it:

1. *T*ension.
2. *R*esistance.
3. *A*rrogant aggressiveness.
4. *N*egation as a way of life.
5. *Q*uandary.
6. *U*nbelief.
7. *I*nferiority.
8. *L*ife of loneliness.
9. *L*aissez-faire.
10. *I*rritation.
11. *T*repidation.
12. *Y*esterday Incorporated.

Succumb to these negative forces and you will never know what tranquillity is. Combat these forces, overcome these destructive forces, and then your voyage will be under way: toward the land of tranquillity.

1. Tension. Tranquillity and tension are opposites; they cannot coexist. Life brings with it problems and tensions, but stresses and strains are there for you to overcome, not to retain as a way of life. You can look at tensions as stimuli giving you creative opportunities to prove yourself and find renewed respect for yourself. With an active approach to living, you move through life's tensions to your goals; then, with tension shrugged aside, you can relax.

Change creates tension because people must readjust to newness, and this is always difficult. Change is so rapid in our swift-moving world, vibrating to the constant dynamism of our complex technology and its multifaceted products, that many people give in to the tension habit.

Above and beyond the load of tensions that we cannot avoid we burden ourselves with unnecessary tension; we worry about things that never happen and bury ourselves in obsessive anxieties. We take a passive view of life's uncertainties. This passivity renders us helpless to forces we cannot cope with; so that we can only tie ourselves up with tension in our helplessness.

To overcome tension, you must take a more active approach to living. Wake up in the morning and think of something constructive to brighten your day. Then get off your back and, fighting off your worries and your doubts, get out into the world and live the best way you can. After a good go at your goals, you are ready for your trip to the good land— tranquillity.

2. Resistance. Resistance can be positive. Take, for example, the "resistance movements" that were organized in France and other European countries during World War II to oppose the Nazi tyranny by slowing down troop movements, blowing up bridges and railroad tracks, and hiding and protecting people the Nazis wanted to kill.

When your resistance consists of negation of your successful goal-directedness, you produce only frustration and destroy not your enemy, but your emotional friend—tranquillity. When the French Resistance in the early 1940s dynamited a train full of Nazi war munitions bound for the front, saving the lives of American doughboys, that was a good thing; when you sabotage your worthwhile daily goals, placing roadblocks all around you in resistance of your legitimate satisfactions, that is not so good.

For your peace of mind, you must fight off your own self-defeating resistance to your worthwhile plans. You must appreciate that you have rights, that you are deserving, and that you are a decent human being with an overpowering need for happiness. You are not inferior and unworthy. You must not stop yourself in your tracks with the crippling negation of your inner resistance to your growth.

When you overcome your resistance, cast off your chains and reject your prison, you can travel to the golden land of tranquillity.

3. Arrogant aggressiveness. We all need aggressiveness to move toward our goals. When you move toward goals which are within your training and your other capacities and which are socially constructive, your aggressiveness in pursuing these goals serves you well. Indeed, this constructive type of aggressiveness spurs you on to achievements.

But arrogant aggressiveness is a different kettle of fish. It is asking for trouble—and trouble is what you'll get.

The arrogantly aggressive individual is ruthless and inconsiderate. He will tolerate no interference with his goals; he cares nothing for other people's feelings and will step on their toes or crush their egos with his dominating personality to reach his goals. In his arrogance, he recognizes no limitations; in a sense he's a baby reaching for his bottle, he wants that bottle and will raise an earth-shaking commotion if he does not get it and now.

This arrogant type of aggressiveness naturally disturbs the equilibrium of other people; it then rebounds from others back to the initiator of all the trouble. Thus arrogant aggressiveness leads to all-round chaos.

Thus tranquillity begins when you learn the difference between taking from life and giving to life. When you learn to give to life you will be able to take happiness from life, because happiness belongs to you. You will also give consideration to other people, because happiness belongs to them too. Your aggression will be goal-directed and constructively channeled—not an exercise in ruthlessness or unbounded egotism.

4. Negation as a way of life. Will this lead to tranquillity? Of course not. Anyone can see that. But is your vision clear —or is it blurred?

I met a man who had "blurred vision."

His wife phoned me recently. She said, "I'd like to see you with my husband. He has blurred vision."

"Well, that's not my. . . ."

"He was just examined by specialists," she went on. "They found nothing wrong with his eyes."

"Oh?"

The words poured out, overflowing. "We love each other. I read your book *Psycho-Cybernetics*. We have our children. The last one was a Caesarean. I studied for the opera."

"All right," I said. "You're going too fast for me. Why don't you and your husband come to see me?"

And there they were, opposite me. He was slim, in his early forties; she was shorter and stockier. They talked about themselves. He was an engineer. He said he liked his job, but he kept insisting he could get more pay if he switched. She had studied singing for many years. She had always loved to sing, but had made no professional appearances.

"How long have you had blurred vision?" I asked.

"Two years."

"Tell me about yourself. About your background."

She answered for him. "His mother died when she gave birth to him, and his father died when he was two. His grandma took care of him. He told me when he did something wrong, his grandma would not hit him; instead she hit her own head against the wall."

"And you? What about your singing?"

He answered for her. "It's my fault."

"Why?"

"We met in Germany years ago. We were married. One child came, then another."

"The last one was a Caesarean," she said.

"I love my wife," he said, "and my children. But I'm not happy."

"He doesn't feel he deserves to be happy," she claimed.

"I see trouble ahead of us," he said. "I always worry about what will happen. I keep worrying about everything. I don't relax very much. Maybe we'll go back to Germany. I can get a job in West Berlin for five thousand dollars a year—maybe I'll take it. But I don't know. Maybe I shouldn't."

I handed him a book. "Can you read this page to me?"

"It's blurred," he said.

"But the eye doctor said there was nothing wrong with your eyes?"

"He found nothing wrong."

"I find something wrong," I said.

"You do?"

"But not with your eyes."

"What, then?"

"Your image of yourself is blurred—you do not see yourself clearly. You use negation as a way of life. Apparently your eyes are fine—the specialists told you that—but you are still living in the past, blaming yourself for all your painful yesterdays. You probably blame yourself for your mother's death and your father's death, and you keep feeling guilty. And do you blame yourself for your grandmother's hitting her head against the wall?"

He said nothing; he just sighed.

"You keep rejecting happiness and choosing negation," I said. "You blame yourself because your wife had children instead of a singing career. You love your wife and children and yet you bury yourself in yesterday's pains. Then you start dreaming of tomorrow—you'll change jobs, you'll go back to Germany, you'll do this or that—but that ends up in negativism too. You have a yesterday-tomorrow complex—and it's all negative. You see images of yesterday and tomorrow—and they lead you only to negation. Your image of today is blurred; that is what is blurred."

"What should I do?"

"See today," I said, "and live for today. To focus your

vision, look for a happy today. Forget the painful images of your past and your fantasy images of your tomorrow; concentrate on today, every day, and do your best every day to defeat your negative feelings and create happy days for yourself and your family *now.*"

He nodded.

"Now. Today. Those are your key words. Not yesterday. Not tomorrow. Now."

Incidentally, I heard from this man about a year later. His vision was no longer blurred.

Back to you, reading this book: How is your vision? Do you seek tranquillity, or is your vision blurred?

5. *Quandary.* You may spend your life in a constant quandary; many people do. Your days are unfinished symphonies of indecision. You stop and start; you turn around. Who is that worried-looking fellow staring at you? Oh, it's you. You saw yourself in the mirror.

The hard-to-face reality is that many of your decisions will be extremely difficult. You will suffer through the twin tensions of conflict and uncertainty; indecisive, you may find yourself in a continual quandary, wandering around in circles, searching for your sense of direction.

The Louisiana Purchase—now that was a bargain! For $15 million, the United States bought from France an enormous mass of land—room for fourteen new states. Overnight, with this fantastic purchase, the United States was almost doubled in size, extended through the Mississippi Valley and west to the Rocky Mountains. It was perhaps the greatest real estate bargain in history; our nation bought all this land at a price of about two cents an acre. Napoleon felt he had to sell cheap. His troops had been disastrously defeated in Haiti and, giving up his dreams of empire in the Americas, he sold us the Louisiana territories at bargain-basement prices. The decision was then in the hands of the United States government: We bought the territories from France in April 1803. A good decision. But an easy one—and this is my point. A very easy decision. A fantastic bargain. A rare, almost once-in-a-lifetime opportunity.

Just as the United States, as a nation, must ordinarily make decisions of much greater complexity, drawing hairline conclusions and weighing all sides with great care, so must we, as individuals, make many difficult decisions—every year, every month, perhaps every day.

Do we then spend our time in a quandary? Are we never to know what it is like to feel peace of mind?

No, we achieve tranquillity by transforming a destructive quandary into a constructive certainty. We do this by accepting ourselves when we make poor decisions as well as when we make wise decisions. We do this by looking at our failures with kind eyes and by consigning them to the past where they belong. We do this by building an image of ourselves that will stand up under trying conditions. We do this by seeing our full potential as human beings.

6. *Unbelief.* Another non-component of tranquillity is unbelief. When you do not believe in yourself, you waste great amounts of precious time trying to imitate others. This is a great destroyer of inner tranquillity: carrying someone else's image in your imagination; giving someone else this power in your mind when this power rightfully belongs to you.

Unbelief is a passive attitude stemming from self-doubt and leading to defeat and despair. Doubt comes from error, and when you decide to forgive yourself and forget yesterday's errors, focusing instead on the confidence of your past successes, you take a giant step toward destroying unbelief and laying the foundations for peace of mind.

7. *Inferiority.* When you walk around day in day out, feeling a sense of inferiority eating away inside you, obviously you cannot know what it feels like to attain tranquillity.

So you must out-wrestle this self-dooming sense of inferiority; you must throw off this blanket of gloom that keeps you passive to a world in which you make other people superior to you.

Are others as superior as you think they are? No, they are just people—people with problems and anxieties and eccentricities, some of which they try to hide from you so you won't think they are inferior.

Why do you see them as superior? Because you make mountains of your mistakes. Because you cannot forgive yourself for your human imperfections. Because your enormous and surely unreasonable guilt chokes off your creative self-expression, and you punish yourself constantly for your mountainous mistakes. You feel, then, if you do this, that since you are so worthless, other people by comparison are superior to you.

Furthermore, since you feel you are so inferior, you may carry this inner destructiveness out into inadequate performance in the world. Thus you may reinforce your inferiority complex, as you prove the inferiority of your image in life.

To alleviate this self-destructiveness and move toward the land of tranquillity, you must forgive yourself for your mistakes—past, present, and future. You must develop more human attitudes toward yourself. Tell yourself you deserve another chance. Wouldn't you say that to a friend?

8. Life of loneliness. You feel lonely sometimes when you are in a crowd of people—just as you can feel a substantial feeling of brotherly warmth when you are alone. Thus loneliness is a feeling, not a physical state.

Loneliness is also a feeling of dread—you are separate, you are cut off, you must cope with the pain of your sense of isolation.

But, as the late Wendell Willkie insisted, we are One World. Even before our modern jets and spaceships we were, in a sense, one world. European culture through the centuries is a prime example of how cultures influence each other. Europeans learned much of Greek science from the Arabs. The mariner's compass came from China. Other inventions that helped revolutionize European culture were the spinning wheel from India, and the hot-air turbine from Tibet.

Just as European culture was no isolated phenomenon, you too are no island. You are more than an individual—you are also a member of human society. At times you may separate yourself, to feel your unique selfhood more fully, but for peace of mind you must also feel a sense of brotherhood —and perhaps of identification—with other people.

9. Laissez-faire. I do not mean the economic philosophy urging a governmental policy of non-interference, but rather your attitude of accepting things as they are—an overly passive attitude. You don't even try to change things.

You may think that such a non-interfering and "laissez-faire" attitude toward life brings tranquillity, but it does not. It brings passiveness, apathy and inertia—not the same thing as tranquillity at all.

Contrary to what many people think, you must adopt an active approach toward tranquillity. You must work for it.

You must fight for it. You must want it very much. You must move toward your goals; you must keep fighting for them; you do not give up easily. You feel your energy bubbling in you as you move. Then, when you stop driving and relax, you are truly tranquil.

10. Irritation. A disease of the age? A symptom of our "age of anxiety"? Maybe so—but maybe irritation has always been a precondition to living.

Either way, my point is this: We must consider how to handle our irritation.

We cannot run and hide. You will always meet people who will irritate you. You will always face situations which will irritate you.

What do you do?

You utilize the healing power of forgiveness. After you have tried your hardest to make the best of your irritation, and your continuing irritation is only a form of self-destruction, you forgive. You forgive others; and you forgive yourself. There may have been considerable provocation, but you forgive and forget.

As you do, you move toward the cool green pastures of tranquillity.

11. Trepidation. In the chronic sense, trepidation means anxiety as a way of life: Tranquillity-minus—as in the case of a young woman who came to my office not too long ago.

She was a beautiful woman, married, in her early twenties. Before she married, she had been the beauty queen of her country, Santo Domingo. Life had been good to her.

Then, suddenly, it happened. While riding in a car that her husband, a financier, was driving, there was a terrible collision. The husband and six-year-old daughter escaped injury. But the wife suffered a terrible deep wound of her cheek running into the angle of her mouth and the skin over the left nostril was torn from her face.

She burst into tears as she told me her story. She had lived in despair since then. Many times she had thought of suicide. She forgot how to laugh. How could she regain the inner peace she had once known?

In the operating room, she was placed under general anesthesia, and I began to repair the damage. I removed the scar tissue of the cheek, undermined the opposing edges of the wound, and approximated the skin edges with interrupted sutures of fine silk. The angle of the mouth was now normal —so was the tissue of the cheek. Except for the stitches, both cheeks were once again symmetrical. A circular piece of skin about the size of a nickel was removed from behind her left ear and grafted into place over the nostril defect; it was kept in place with interrupted sutures of silk.

Ten days later came the big day; time to remove the final dressings; time for the fearful confrontation.

She was the picture of dread. She insisted that she would not look in the mirror. I coaxed her. Finally, she looked— apprehensively. Then, joy swept over her, and she wept.

"I thought I'd never be myself again," she cried.

"But you are," I said.

She kissed her husband. She kissed her daughter. She even kissed me. We all laughed. The cloud of trepidation was gone.

I do not really tell this dramatic story for illustrative purposes. I tell it for comparison, to help you who must overcome the emotional scars—not the physical ones—that cause so much anxiety in people. You must be your own emotional plastic-surgeon. With compassion for yourself, you must forgive. Your emotional scars are invisible—not as in the dramatic case of the beauty queen—but they may cause you chronic consternation. You remove them when you forgive yourself for your past thoughts, for your past actions, and for all the mistakes of yesterday. When you have successfully removed your emotional scars, you will begin to live in the present—with tranquillity.

12. Yesterday Incorporated. I have written, in *Creative Living for Today*, about mañana-type thinking. The members of Mañana Incorporated have dedicated themselves to delaying almost everything until tomorrow. Their belief in "tomorrow" is so fervent that they never do anything today.

The members of Yesterday Incorporated also do nothing, or very little, today. They live in the past, not the future—but the result is the same: very little creative living today.

Recently a lovely woman, married and in her early thirties, came to my office. She was beautiful, but her eyes mirrored a deep sadness.

She told me about her father, and how she had loved him. He had died four months before, and she grieved for his passing. She insisted, again and again, that she could not get over her father's death.

"He was a poet, a philosopher, a great man of the Bible," she sobbed. "He was such a fine liberal man—so compassionate. I loved him so much."

She told me about her husband, a high school teacher of French, and her two children, a boy and a girl. But inevitably she returned to her father. "I married out of my faith, but my father understood."

"Is your mother alive?"

"She lives in Jerusalem."

"Permanently?"

"I hope so."

"What do you mean by that?"

"I can't get along with her. She was against my marriage. She complains all the time. She always complains about her health, but there is nothing physically wrong with her. I think she plans to come back to New York, but I don't know how to get along with her. I miss my father."

"You want my advice?"

"Yes. I've read your philosophy; it is simple, easy to understand, compassionate—it is as if you were writing about my father."

"That's fine," I said. "But you must understand that you can't live in yesterday. To have peace of mind, you must live today. It's wonderful that you love your father, but you can't keep living in the yesterday when he was alive, protecting you, inspiring you. You can't hide behind your father of yesterday away from your mother of yesterday. Respect the memory of your father—but live your own life today. He would have wanted you to. That is the way to reward him—and yourself. Live today."

You, too—if you are a member—resign from Yesterday Incorporated. This corporation has no earnings, declares no dividends, and is headed for bankruptcy; so resign. You will find the land of tranquillity only when you live for today.

Tranquillity: An Active Concept

I have spelled out the roadblocks that keep you from tranquillity. You must defeat these negative forces in order to make your voyage to the land of tranquillity.

You will notice that—as with sincerity and forgiveness—I look upon tranquillity as an active concept. Many people connect tranquillity with lying passively in a hammock, rocking gently, stirring yourself only to brush a fly from your nose or to answer the call for dinner.

I do not agree with this. I see the passive person as one who, in his inertia, makes himself helpless to cope with life's dynamisms and therefore lives with fear and uncertainty, not tranquillity. I don't really refer to the occasional hammock-user who enjoys resting there now and then.

The person who moves toward tranquillity is the constructively aggressive, goal-oriented individual—brotherly in a doing sense—because he gives himself the weapons with which he can master his destiny.

Change does not unsettle him because, reacting to life with an active philosophy, he moves out to deal with change and to adjust to it in a successful way. Thus he is able to live with tranquillity even in an era of rapid change—even in our swiftly moving twentieth century.

Serene, quietly confident, he moves to cement the positive orientation of his life. Calmly, he builds his house brick by brick—and no fleeting wind can knock it down.

Actively, with faith in his powers to create and to make decisions; in his reality and in his mind, he manufactures for himself that greatest of nonmaterial products: tranquillity. As a by-product, proud of himself and of his creation, he also creates self-respect.

Tranquillity—and self-respect.

CHAPTER 12

The Active Life:
No Retirement Clock

WHEN you search for your self-respect, one thing you cannot do is retire from life. This is inconsistent with self-respect. When you throw in the sponge, you throw away your dignity. Retreating from life's battlefields, resigning your commission in the great human army, you are then a traitor to yourself and render yourself vulnerable to attack and defeat by onrushing hordes of negative feelings.

In the last chapter, I wrote about a man with "blurred vision," who needed to refocus his emotional forces. Well, people who retire from life also suffer from "blurred vision." People with foresight stand up to life's problems and, though they may seek physical or emotional solitude now and then they rally their inner strength and return to a sense of full participation. Like General Douglas MacArthur, they come back to win.

Or at least they try.

No retirement clock for them—they prefer self-respect. What is a retirement clock? Is it the clock that chimes out the age of sixty-five, ushering you into a land of rocking chairs and soft cushions?

No. I have written enough about the perils of age sixty-five. I have written many pages about the quicksand philosophy with which too many people doom themselves at sixty-five, dragging themselves down to an inner death as they tell themselves that they are too "old" to do anything or have any fun.

No, this retirement clock is a mechanism that knows no distinctions of age. For people may withdraw from life at five or fifteen as well as at sixty-five.

There is a retirement clock in all of us. It ticks away useless seconds, useless minutes, useless hours. It ticks away in people of all age when, submerging themselves in negative feelings, they waste their precious time in worry, frustration, and retirement—from life and from their sense of aliveness.

Our world is fast-moving and time is a key element in our lives. How could it work without clocks—in airport terminals, railroad stations, savings banks, telegraph offices, mass-production factories, and department stores?

In the home, too. What kind of clock do you have in your home? Is it electric, or do you have to wind it up? Is it an alarm clock? A grandfather's clock, ticking away? Or do you have a wrist watch? Is that the "clock" in your home?

It really doesn't matter—just so it tells the time, just so it keeps you in tune with the world.

The worst clock in the world is your retirement clock. A stop-watch doesn't really stop you. You may use it to temporarily "freeze" time and show how fast your friend can run. Your retirement clock however can stop you. If the ticking of your retirement clock hypnotizes you, pulls you away from your belief in yourself and in the world of people, and draws you away into a desert where nothing grows, you must cast off its influence and escape from the monotony of its beat. You need an alarm clock to ring out harshly, awakening you from your stupor, shrieking out against your inertia, warning you that you must wake up to the meaning of life—which is living.

You need an alarm clock to summon you from a life of sleepwalking to a life of constructive doing, to bring you back to a concentration on your goals, to shock you into movement toward life, and to jet-propel you from vague dreams to stark reality.

I have long felt that most people do not really understand the meaning of self-respect.

Self-respect does not mean perfection. It does not mean complete realization of all your dreams. It does not mean that you are better than everybody else. It does not mean anything ideal, absolute, or all-powerfull.

Self-respect means this: You seek and you search. You do your best. You are sincere in your desire to make yourself the best kind of person you can. You accept yourself as you are, with all your limitations, and accept other people too, with compassion and brotherliness. You forgive others, and yourself, in an active sense, making your forgiveness real—in action as well as in thought.

When you exercise your resources, day after day, week after week, developing yourself as a human being, reaching out to other people in friendliness, moving toward constructive goals in your world, overcoming your negative feelings to feel more life, refusing to let external defeats and your own mistakes stop you, relishing life's daily challenges— then you feel self-respect.

Then no retirement clock inside you ticks away minutes of withdrawal from life.

Then you fight off the guilts of yesterday, and the fantasies of tomorrow.

You must stop accusing yourself of past crimes; you must refuse to let past mistakes force you into self-hate and panicky withdrawal from life.

And tomorrow?

Stop fantasizing about tomorrow also; live today.

Live in your precious hours and minutes and seconds. Now is the time for living. There must be no retirement clock.

Retirement or Living: Your Choice

You have a choice: retirement from life or full living. This is your problem; this is your choice. You are on the fence; which way will you jump?

The retirement mechanism—or clock—ticks away emptiness. We will now examine and spell out its components along with their opposites, giving you both sides of the coin in one toss.

1. *R*etreat	RETURN
2. *E*viction	CONVICTION
3. *T*endency to withdraw	COURAGE TO ACT
4. *I*mpotence	IMAGINATIVE POWER
5. *R*esignation	REAFFIRMATION
6. *E*vasion	RESPONSIBILITY
7. *M*añana	TODAY
8. *E*nnui	EMANCIPATION
9. *N*o direction	GOAL ORIENTATION
10. *T*raitor	FRIEND

Retirement: an enemy to avoid. These are the components of the retirement mechanism, of the retirement clock, which ticks away emptiness and despair. Alongside them you also find your alternatives, the components of a rich life, components that bring you closer to your feelings of success.

Now let us first examine the dangers you must skirt, one by one. Then let us examine your alternatives, which direct you toward fuller living and self-respect.

1. Retreat. (The alternative is: Return.) This is the fundamental concept of retirement. You presuppose a dangerous, threatening world; as soon as you can, you retreat from it. You walk away from its problems and its responsibilities; if you are truly frightened, you run away.

You find much evidence to support your stand. The world is difficult; it changes too fast; people are always fighting with each other; you can't win.

And so you retreat. You move away from people. You keep to yourself. You go into hiding.

Now I cannot deny that critics of our world score with some of their attacks. Certainly the world is difficult, anyway. But you can win.

I say to you: Retreat if you must—but then return.

Life is never a series of smoothly flowing victories. Everyone knows defeat and despair. But the fighters, the battlers struggling to fulfill their potentials, they return.

As did Richard Nixon, who survived crushing political setbacks and returned—to become President of the United States.

As did the late Franklin Delano Roosevelt, who survived physical misfortune and returned—to lead our nation out of economic depression.

As did the ballplayers on the New York Mets, for years characterized as one of the most inept teams in baseball history, who returned in 1969 to play each game one at a time, living for the day, until they had amazingly climbed the ladder to the top.

Life may seem tough to you, problems endless, obstacles insurmountable. You feel tired and defeated. But keep going; and, following the example of the 1969 New York Mets, underrated and chronic losers, return—to win.

2. Eviction. (The alternative is: Conviction.) Are you a victim of eviction? That is, have you instituted eviction proceedings against yourself from the world? From life? From the world of people?

Have you so completely evicted yourself from yourself, having no faith in your own powers, that you flee from a world in which everyone seems so superior to you because you feel so inferior?

Many people do evict themselves, saying they cannot help it, they have had bad breaks, no one ever befriended them, they are inferior.

Maybe they have had bad breaks.

Recently I read about a study of an orphanage in Teheran. Whereas most children sit up alone at about ten months, sixty percent of these orphaned children could not sit up alone at the age of two years. While most children learn to walk alone at about fourteen or fifteen months, 85 percent of these orphans could not walk alone at the advanced age of four years.

Now obviously many of these children were severely handicapped at the beginning of their lives, slow starters. Here is real misfortune.

But what would you say to them, victims of really bad breaks: Give up? You can't win? Don't even try? It's not worth it?

No, sir. This is eviction, and it is destructive. Deprived children may have to face the reality of their limitations, but must they be forced to face a life without hope?

Conviction is the answer. Belief in oneself. These orphaned children—or you—maybe you can't do everything and maybe you're not perfect and maybe some people can outcompete you in some areas and maybe you're not even a little omnipotent. Still, you feel inside yourself a conviction.

You know as a certainty that you do your best and, beyond any shadow of a doubt, you know that you don't give up easily.

Further, it is your strong conviction that your goals are worthwhile.

And you move toward life with conviction; no eviction for you.

3. Tendency to withdraw. (*The alternative is: Courage to act.*) Once again, another "moving-away" symptom—a failure-oriented tendency. This is a reaction to a feeling that life is too tough; it represents helplessness and panic as a way of life.

You must overcome this tendency, if you have it, with all your determination. You must develop the courage to act, even in very trying circumstances, even when you're frightened, even when you make mistakes and feel foolish or alarmed.

I have my disagreements with some of the existentialist philosophers, but I must agree with their emphasis on a person's facing life, exercising responsibility, making choices.

In my own theory of psycho-cybernetics, I stress the concept that, valuable as positive thinking is and it is extremely valuable, you must go beyond positive thinking and develop the courage to act—with constructive goals in mind.

In creative psycho-cybernetics, you combat your fearful tendencies by refocusing on your past successes, making your happy moments live again in your imagination, over and over, fortifying your sense of self-esteem, so that you can reverse your orientation toward failure and build in yourself the courage to act constructively.

4. Impotence. (The alternative is: Imaginative power.) Lack of power, lack of drive. Everyone feels impotent sometimes, that's nothing. But when you feel impotent day after day, week after week, that's something else.

Nobody can exercise a steady control on all areas of his life all the time. This does not indicate *im*potence, but lack of *omni*potence. We should recognize this and understand that when things go wrong for a while, we should not withdraw from the world and from ourselves. We should stay in the world, with its winds and its rain and its lightning and thunder—until we weather the storm.

A short story about a good friend of mine: She came to New York from a small town. Her family was large—many brothers and sisters—and the church played a big role in the life of the community.

She got a good job. She built a fine life for herself in the big city.

Then, one afternoon, she thought of the small town in which she had grown up—and of the church. She wanted to do good. She would send the church a check for fifty dollars.

She did. A check was sent from a big-town girl to a home-town priest.

Fifty dollars.

Five thousand pennies for heaven.

And it bounced.

She told me about it, embarrassed. She had only wanted to do good. But she had forgotten to add up her checking balance. Temporarily, she felt powerless. She deposited more money in her account and sent the check out again, but for a few days she felt she could do nothing good until the church received her new check. Until then she felt a spiritual impotence—as if nothing could go right with the world.

What do you do when you feel this way? Friend, stay with it! Use your imagination to help you out. Let your imaginative power pull you to your feet—with images of your past successes to help tide you through your period of emotional impotence.

5. Resignation. (The alternative is: Reaffirmation.) Your life is bleak. Your wife screamed at you as you left, your boss screamed at you at the office, the traffic cop screamed at you as you drove home (and gave you a ticket). You are batting 100 percent—all wrong.

What do you do? Resign from your job? Divorce your wife? Do you tear up your driving license? Renounce your citizenship? Resign from the human race?

No, you reaffirm. You reaffirm your belief in yourself (no matter what others think). You reaffirm your rights—to happiness, to pleasure, to self-respect. You reaffirm.

In ancient Rome, toasts were a common formality. The people customarily pledged the health of their friends as they drank their wine. Then the Roman Senate decreed that diners toast the health of Augustus at all gatherings. Surely there was much pledging of good health in those times.

Reaffirmation? Of a sort, I guess, but not quite what I had in mind for you. When you feel low, when you feel depressed, when you feel like resigning from life, bestow on yourself a liquorless toast. Pledge yourself richness in living, reaffirm your faith in yourself, get back in the ring and start punching.

6. *Evasion. (The alternative is: Responsibility.)* You can spend your lifetime being evasive, but where will it get you? You can hide, and you can run away; but where?

There is no absolute justice in life. So, how do you react to life's inequities?

I jotted down some statistics on the education of women. One 1966 study showed that women's presence in our labor force was related to her education; that the more educated woman was more likely in the labor force. According to this study, 45 percent of women who had graduated from high school only were in the labor force or looking, compared to 53 percent with four years of college, and 72 percent with five or more years of higher education.

Another study, of gifted college students, indicated that about 50 percent more gifted women than men dropped out of college.

Both studies indicate inequities, though along different lines. I will not analyze them. That is not my concern here.

My point is this: Assuming that these statistics apply to you, or identifying with them in some fashion, with yours the sub-par status, how do you react?

With the feeling that life is not worthwhile, so why not run away and hide?

Or with the determination that come what may you will hang in there, take your punches, and continue to accept your responsibilities in our imperfect world?

The choice is yours, but accepting reality and responsibility leads you away from the destructive retirement mechanism to self-respect.

7. *Mañana.* (*The alternative is: Today.*) When you keep putting things off for mañana (tomorrow), you never do them; in your nondoing you retire from the realities of life.

Today. That's the word for real living. Today.

Recently I delivered some lectures in Miami Beach. At one, I spoke to six hundred women, and before my lecture they had a raffle. Some women won perfume, a hairdo set, a radio, and some won fine silverware. Others, of course, won nothing.

You take a chance when you bet on a raffle. When you live in the present, you also take a chance. But the rewards are great—when you participate, when you are involved, when you are a doer.

Still, that's the road to self-respect. Living for today. Not for mañana.

8. *Ennui.* (*The alternative is: Emancipation.*) Ennui means boredom, and boredom means you're only half alive. You're not collecting Social Security or any form of pension, and maybe you're still in your teens or twenties, but you are retired.

The powerful boa constrictor eats, sleeps, and keeps right on sleeping until once again hungry.

Not much of a life. If you'll permit me a small joke, not much pressure.

To rise above ennui, you must feel a sense of emancipation. Emancipation—the freedom to feel confidence in yourself and live without unreasonable and constricting guilt crushing your spirit, a boa constrictor crushing your bones.

Free yourself from the past, from the guilts that torture you and the mistakes that haunt you. You deserve to live, a free human being, today.

9. No direction. (The alternative is: Goal orientation.) If you have no direction, you feel empty. Each day is a dilemma because you are aimless: there is no goal, no movement, no sense of achievement. Soon you do nothing at all. You end up retiring from life.

With goal orientation, your sense of being alive bubbles. You are no longer asleep; you wake up to the opportunities around you. Your sleepwalking is in the past; today is what is important. Your goals bring you out of your daily retirement into a life of meaning.

As I write this, the great cellist Pablo Casals, although over ninety years old, is still a young man. Because he lives for the day. In a recent interview, Casals told a reporter how each day he is born again to live a new lifetime. Casals has lived more than ninety years of goals and excitement. This is real living.

10. Traitor. (The alternative is: Friend.) Concluding this discussion of the negation of retirement from life, I suggest that you ask yourself this: Are you "traitor" or "friend" to yourself?

When you retire from life—and from your image of yourself—you are truly a "traitor" to yourself.

You need all the friends you can get, as the saying goes, and there is realistically one friend you must have—yourself.

Befriend yourself, and never retire.

The Generation Gap

Now let me tell you a story. We have spelled out the destructive retirement-mechanism—the retirement clock—and the life forces with which you can oppose it, in young and old. This story, too, is about young and old; it is about what I might call a "generationless gap."

A quiet, friendly, gray-haired man in his sixties came to see me. He was an engineer, of Swedish extraction. He came from New Jersey to talk about his problem with his son, twenty-three years old, unmarried, and who lived with him.

He had two other sons; they were married. He was worried only about his youngest son. They never talked to each other after "hello" and "goodbye." What should he do about it?

It was a strange meeting, in that I repeatedly found myself forming interpretations which were then suddenly shattered.

The first came quickly—"generation gap," I thought—but later I thought of this as a "generationless gap."

Shortly, I asked him about his wife, and he told me a most unusual story.

Years before, he said, his wife had said to him, "I'm going back to Sweden," packed her valise, and left.

Eight or nine months later, she was back—for two months, then back to Sweden.

It turned out that she had left for Sweden because an elderly man, of eighty, had invited her to live with him in Sweden. She had met this man in New York.

A pattern set in: Each year she went to Sweden for most of the year, and then she came back to her family for two months or so.

"What a terrible problem this man has," I thought to myself.

Of course it was, but, to my surprise, the man's problem did not seem to be with himself at all. He evidenced little sense of being rejected. He accepted the situation, unconventional as it was, and did not want a divorce.

"Would you take her back for good?" I asked.

"Would I, yes! The trouble is with the boys."

"What do you mean?"

"This man is eighty," he said. "If he died, I would take her back. I would feel sorry for her."

I marveled at his compassion for a woman who had basically, left him. "What's that about the boys?" I said.

"They think we're both doing what's best for us. They accept the way things are."

Another preconception destroyed. I had pictured the boys seriously disturbed by their broken home. "But you indicated the trouble was with the boys?"

"The youngest boy."

"What is the problem?"

"Oh, I don't know. He doesn't talk to me."

"Why not?"

"Oh, I don't know."

"You have no idea?"

"Nope."

"Do you think it has something to do with your wife leaving you to go to Sweden?"

"Maybe."

"Your youngest son is twenty-three, you told me. What kind of work does he do?"

"He has no job."

"He's unemployed?"

"Yes."

"Does this bother you?"

"Now and then."

The man was friendly, but not very talkative. Words just didn't come easily for him. I would see his son, I thought.

The boy was another surprise. The father had made him

sound lazy; instead, he was an alert, good-looking six-footer. He wanted to get a job in the banking business; he had confidence he would get what he wanted.

"Why don't you talk to your father?" I asked.

"Oh, I just don't."

"Is it because you don't respect him? Because of what your mother did?"

"Oh, no. I respect Dad."

"Does he keep telling you what to do? Does he pester you because you don't have a job?"

"I want a job."

"Does he blame you because your brothers are married and you're still living with him?"

"Nope."

"Do you have a girl friend?"

"Yes. For three months."

"Do you want to get married?"

"Yes."

"And you don't hate your father because he's dominating you?"

"Nope."

"Or because he's weak, because your mother left and he just takes her back?"

"Nope."

"And he doesn't try to force you any way?"

"Nope. Dad's a great guy."

And, looking into the boy's friendly eyes, remembering the father's friendly eyes, with mounting surprise I realized that once again my preconception was false. This was no "generation gap" brought about by the hatred between generations. This was a "generationless gap."

Its cause: like father, like son. The father didn't talk much, and the son didn't talk much. They didn't hate each other; the father was perhaps a little worried about his son, but there was little if any hate. The son really liked the father. Their trouble was that they did not know how to communicate, that their shyness and clipped speech operated as destructive barriers which separated them from each other, bringing about an enforced retirement.

No hatred operated here, but a retirement clock which ticked away in both men: Minutes and hours were wasted. Through mutual ignorance, so common in so many families, they sat silent, withdrawing from each other though they wanted to be close.

I talked to the son about the importance of opening up lines of communication with his father. I told him it was his responsibility—he was younger. I stressed that he had to gather up the courage to do this; that this was a goal of major importance in his life.

I felt that father and son had learned from me—I hope they learned as much from me as I learned from them.

The Active Life and Self-Respect

Which brings me back to an earlier point: The retirement clock is the worst clock in the world. It ticks away wasted time and it respects no generations. It ticks away in young and old alike.

In this chapter we have spelled out the destructive components of the retirement mechanism and we have stressed the positive forces which you can harness to overcome the negatives which would pull you away from full living.

My theory of creative psycho-cybernetics involves an active approach. I believe in an active life, with goals and with enthusiasms. I believe in constructive thinking and imaging, and doing. I believe in full living each day, even though this may mean that, since you are less protected than if you remained passive, you may make mistakes every day.

With an active approach, moving toward living and doing rather than away from it, I feel that you reach out toward your most complete sense of self-respect.

One of your great comforts is that you accept your mistakes; you live amiably with them; you refuse to expect perfection of yourself.

This comforting cushion enables you to come out of your shell, secure in the knowledge that you will give yourself compassion and understanding when you need it. Then you no longer need to listen to the ticking of the retirement clock; because inhibiting fear and crippling self-reproach are muted, you do not waste time worrying obsessively about your actions in the world.

You exercise sensible caution when necessary, but you refuse to coddle yourself. You refuse also to retire from life's problems and life's anxieties and life's uncertainties.

In an active sense, you do your best to make yourself the best human being you can be. What a superb goal! It follows naturally that your sense of self-respect will grow.

CHAPTER 13

Integrity as a Way of Life

MANY of us, succumbing to the pressures of our modern technological civilization, live fragmented lives. We rush around in all directions, cornered and misdirected in our confusion, unnerved in our rush to scoop up what we think is good in life, and assuming appropriate facades for self-protection, as we seek to master the many complicated situations we encounter each day.

Too many people lose track of themselves. They probably know where their automobile is; because they have just driven it into the garage. They feel secure about the location of their bankbook; they have a special place for it. Jingling the keys is reassuring; the key to the house or apartment is right there. The key to the mail box, to the automobile, to the safe deposit box, are all present and accounted for. It gives people a good feeling to know that everything is in order. But have they kept in touch with themselves?

In most cases, unfortunately, the answer is no. For many people today are not close to themselves.

A couple of years ago the title of one of my lectures was "The Whole Man: Let's Keep Him Whole." But, come to think of it, I might have rephrased my lecture title and made it "How to Become a Whole Man." Because, though our gross national product statistics are huge and impressive and we are a wealthy nation of hard-working and energetic people, not too many of us are complete people.

But we want to be complete people; and that is our blazing hope. We want to be people of integrity; and that is our saving grace. We seek integrity as a way of life; and this ardent seeking makes us great.

Integrity means wholeness and a man or woman cannot be whole if he or she is internally divided, at war with himself, with herself. The battleground is not only in Vietnam and the Middle East; it is in the heart of every individual who seethes with negative feelings and who builds a thick wall of resentment inside himself, separating himself from himself and from other people. A man can be financially wealthy but if he slashes at himself with negative feelings he is emotionally poverty-stricken. He must negotiate with himself; he must declare a cease-fire; he must move toward integrity as a way of life.

You must keep track of many things to survive. The housewife must remember to turn off the oven, to put out her cigarette, to lock the door when she leaves to go shopping. The breadwinner must remember to pay his taxes, to meet his insurance deadlines, to get to work on time. Functional essentials. You want to survive—so you remember.

But you want to survive as a whole person. You want your integrity; you want your image of yourself to be a support, not a handicap; and you want your self-image to be hearty and expansive, not shrunk to the size of a microbe.

It is self-respect that we seek and a sense of wholeness—or integrity.

Let us keep track of more than our survival functions. We want more out of life than physical survival to an old age. We want to survive whole, and with self-respect. We want to do more than total up years; we want to total years of integrity.

We want to spell out for ourselves a master plan leading to integrity. And that's what we will do now.

The "Grit" in Integrity

This is no easy task. We must all cope with many pressures and conflicting demands. Survival itself may be difficult. Survival with integrity may be an enormous challenge.

Still, if you spell it out, you will find "grit" in "integrity" and this "grit" you must also find in yourself to make yourself whole.

The components of integrity? Let's spell them out now.

1. *I*nquiring mind.
2. *N*atural good tone.
3. *T*houghtful focusing.
4. *E*ncountering the you in you.
5. *G*oal of confidence.
6. *R*eaching for reality.
7. *I*ndustrious involvement.
8. *T*enacity in thinking.
9. *Y*earning for emotional nourishment.

When you go into a restaurant, sit down at a table, and place your order, you hopefully await the return of your waiter with strengthening food. Here, too, we move toward feeding: a basic and strengthening feeding of your capacities for development. Self-service style, though. For you must do more than read; you must want to help yourself.

1. Inquiring mind. What is the great gift that distinguishes you from animals? Your mind. It is a great gift if you use it. But the question remains: Do you use it? Do you use it to make yourself a whole, growing, responsible human being? Or do you let it stagnate?

You cannot touch your mind as you can your skin, but it is there to use. You respond continually to the needs of your skin—in hot weather and cold, in rain and in snow. You bathe and don clothing. You use soap and apply lotions. You never are passive about your skin; you react to any threat and move quickly to protect your skin, which covers your vital organs. What about your mind? Do you use it? Creatively? Inquiringly? Remember this: If you do not use your mind, your mind is useless to you.

Looking in the mirror, you see your face. But, now, go beyond that; use your imagination to see the face of your mind behind your eyes. Ask yourself: What can my mind do? What is its potential? Am I holding it back from operating—with timidity, or fear of making mistakes? How can I exercise my mind so that it will work for me instead of against me? How can I use my mind so that I feel more complete as an individual? Ask yourself these questions.

You can, of course, survive by playing second fiddle all your life, but why not gather up your courage and lead the orchestra? That orchestra plays beautiful music when you use your mind to see your successes instead of your failures.

With an inquiring mind, you see yourself in perspective. You see your past in focus, but you also see your current and future possibilities. Realistically you see yourself as you are— and what you can become. You feel complete as you see the whole picture.

You see other people too. You watch them walking on the sidewalk, talking at restaurant tables, relaxing on planes and trains and buses, browsing in department stores. When you are personally involved with other people, you may not be objective but when, as a stranger, you observe them, you can assess their virtues and their shortcomings. You can learn from their pluses and profit by avoiding their minuses. As human beings, we share many common tendencies. The person with an inquiring mind can give his energies to the rewarding pursuit of self-improvement—every day, in many ways, and all his lfe.

2. Natural good tone. Just as the natural good tone in the muscles of your body may lead to good health, so may the natural good tone in the "muscles" of your mind. How do you achieve this? You do so, once again, by exercise.

People will move heaven and earth to get physical exercise—and with good reason, for it's good for them. They will go through agony for physical exercise. During the summer months, people will get in their cars and head for beaches or lakes, crawling bumper-to-bumper and inch-by-inch for miles until they can break through the city traffic blockages that seem inevitable. Even in the winter, weekend trains are jammed—with skiers and ice skaters. There are also the army of walkers who reject modern technological process in favor of stretching their legs.

Of course, in getting physical exercise, there is a right way and a wrong way. As a very young man shortly after World War I, I learned to bicycle in Amsterdam, Holland. I bicycled everywhere. I even used to follow my professor over narrow lanes and bridges, pedaling to the clinics and to the university. Fine exercise, the right way. But later, on vacation in Bermuda, I tried it the wrong way. Showing off for friends, I took off on my bike down a very, very steep hill, full speed ahead. When I picked myself off the ground, I found I was fortunate—no broken bones.

Physical exercise gives you good natural tone. In stimulating the healthy functioning of your body, you also beef up your feelings of emotional well-being.

Many people swear by setting-up exercises to get their day off to a good start. Breathe in deeply; then breathe out. Exercise mornings for good physical tone.

Natural good tone is also an essential for you on an emotional level. When you wake up in the morning, walk over to a mirror and look at yourself. You've seen that face before—and you'll see it again and again, hopefully—but what you're looking for is a feeling that you're glad you're you and you're glad that you're alive. Over and over as the days pass, aim at giving yourself this good emotional tone each morning, seeing all sides of your personality, striving for self-acceptance and wholeness. Reread Chapter 9 on mirror watching for more detailed ideas on this.

3. Thoughtful focusing. To achieve integrity as a way of life, you must learn to focus with thoughtfulness and concentration on the complexity of your life—your past, present, and future; your limitations and your possibilities—and weave all the strands together into a coherent pattern. Thoughtful focusing means razor-sharp observation in three dimensions: within you, behind you, and before you.

Before we go into this, however, suppose we all try a little experiment. Seat yourself in a large-sized room and try to focus on all the objects in this room. Spend a few minutes, concentrating; your goal is to remember every object in the room. Now walk out of the room and write down every object you can remember. Then re-enter the room and note the objects that slipped your mind. Chances are that you did forget a number of items, for sharp focusing is no easy task. I have tried this exercise on some people, using my living room as the experimental area, and most people overlooked many things.

Why? Because sharp, thoughtful focusing is an art that you develop with practice. Most people appraise superficially and incompletely. So do not expect your three-dimensional appraisal to achieve lightning-quick results for you. Focus thoughtfully, but give yourself time. Develop your perceptiveness with practice.

Each day remember to:

Focus within yourself, taking stock of your assets as well as your liabilities, making an in-depth inventory of yourself, cutting the red tape and the fat, emphasizing your past successes and your positive qualities.

Focus behind yourself, seeing the past to give you perspective on today—not to brood over past mistakes and failures—reminding yourself of past blunders only so that you can avoid repeating them.

Focus before yourself, looking to the great day that lies ahead of you, clearing away the smog and fog with your creative enthusiasm.

4. Encountering the you in you. Integrity means not only wholeness; it means also an impeccable honesty. The person with integrity is trustworthy; he pays his debts and honors his promises; and his word is good.

We are, beyond question, extremely complicated human

beings. We are composites of positive and negative feelings and images. We rise above our failures only with great effort to our full stature as human beings.

This is how you encounter the you within yourself—the you that you like, the you whose integrity is unquestioned, the you whom you respect. It takes great effort and a positively oriented selectivity.

The power of selectivity operates in all of us. The playwright uses his good material and discards the irrelevant as he weaves his plot and moves to the climax of his story. So do you. You are a playwright too, and your drama is the story of your life. The big question is: Do you select the you in you? The you that you like? The you that is sincere, determined, successful? The you with integrity?

In weaving your plot, discard your negative feelings and choose your assets. Build your play around your success feelings. Your stage props are confidence, forgiveness, courage. Your lighting is bright; you have nothing to hide. When the curtain rises and the audience encounters you, you will find that you are well-received.

5. Goal of confidence. Confidence generally leads to a sense of completeness and to honest and equitable relations with other people; so we must list it now, in our analysis of integrity, as a worthy goal.

You develop confidence when you keep your eye on the ball.

When you play golf you keep your eye on the golf ball, then you belt it.

If you don't like the idea of driving for an hour through traffic to the golf course, then try my version of indoor golf in your living room.

Your wife is glaring at you? She is lifting her most expensive vase above her head? She is about to throw it at you?

Reassure your good wife: her furniture is safe. You will play symbolic golf only. No golf clubs, no ball. You will merely imagine that you are playing golf; you will assume the correct golfing stance, keep your eye on the imaginary ball, then follow through.

Silly?

Not at all. This exercise is a basic and worthwhile reminder that to reach your goals you must keep going—all the way to your goal. This is the road to confidence.

Almost everybody has experienced many near-misses: a big business deal that fell through at the last minute, a promotion that almost happened, a nearly successful interview. People with confidence know that they must follow through, keeping their eyes on the ball even though they are tired, until the signature is on the dotted line. This symbolic golf exercise can remind you that you must keep your eye on the ball all the way and follow through completely or you will hit the ball glancingly off to the side and into the trees.

Persistence is the basic answer. How did I become a plastic surgeon? By being persistent and by keeping my eye on the ball, I succeeded.

I grew up on the lower East Side in New York, as I've written, and I survived the numerous perils of a youth living in a rough neighborhood—enjoyed some of them, too. I proceeded with my education and finally decided I wanted to become a doctor.

But it was not until I was about to graduate from medical school that I decided to become a plastic surgeon. I delivered my first child, and it came into the world with a harelip (a hole in the lip). It seemed insufferably cruel for a baby to come into the world disfigured and I made my decision: I would be a plastic surgeon. I would train myself to help human beings born with disfigurements, and those victimized later on, from accidents at home, on the highways, or in industry.

I got little encouragement. My mother, anxious to protect me, afraid I would not make a good living in what was then a little-known specialty, urged me to forget my wild dreams, and become a general practitioner. I asked my professor for advice; he too discouraged me. When I talked to my friends about plastic surgery, I received blank looks as my answer.

But I continued to keep my eye on the ball and follow through. Because I knew what *I* wanted. I overcame a great many obstacles, traveled to Europe to study, and finally returned home to practice plastic surgery.

My situation was still difficult. Many people were critical of what they called beauty surgery. They didn't agree that it was the natural right of every human being to have normal features. Furthermore, they didn't understand that behind the physical disfigurements were serious, inner, emotional scars. I opened my office, but my first patient was a long time in coming.

Nevertheless, I kept my eye on the ball and followed through; and whatever successes I have enjoyed through the years, and whatever confidence I feel, I attribute to this. Today, more than forty years later, people recognize the value of plastic surgery, and almost any good hospital anywhere keeps a capable plastic surgeon on its staff.

Success in our undertakings, and the confidence that follows, is your goal as well as mine.

How do you achieve this?

Through keeping your eye on the ball and following through.

Through your daily game of symbolic golf in your living room.

6. Reaching for reality. Certainly there are vast surpluses of fantasy in people these days—our mass media sees to that. But, to face reality, that is to face yourself with honesty and with a multi-faceted, complex approach—with integrity, in short.

When you reach out for reality, you may experience pain and depression to some extent, but you nevertheless strengthen yourself. The greatest of the ancient philosophers —Socrates, Marcus Aurelius, many others—believed in a realistic approach to self.

There is one hurdle you must jump, however, before you can accept reality. You must learn one great art: the art of forgiveness.

This is not the first time I have mentioned forgiveness in this book, but if you can't forgive yourself for your mistakes, how can you see yourself other than arrogantly—as a person who never makes mistakes?

Of course, you must learn to forgive others too, but first you must learn to forgive yourself.

Then you can develop the capacity for sincerity. But remember this: sincerity is strengthening, whereas insincerity produces exhaustion.

We go through life taxing our physical equipment to its limits. We run here and there; we never seem to have enough time. We even bolt our food on the run, producing the indigestion and other gastric complaints so characteristic of our age.

But equally exhausting is insincerity. Indeed, insincerity is the mother of exhaustion. People who spend their lives putting on airs, blowing up the balloons of their egos, live in constant danger. Someone may take a pin and, as with a balloon, poof! there go their egos. People who spend their lives fencing, shadowboxing, waging cold war after cold war—what is left to them but to crawl back home exhausted from their arduous life of dodging reality.

The wholesome way to life is reaching out to reality. You do not exhaust yourself; you fortify your energy when you face up to the facts, even when they are unpleasant.

Of course, you can go to the other extreme too. Instead of dodging reality, crawling into a womb of fantasy, you can confront yourself with all the most morbid facts all the time, destroying your peace of mind.

A lovely girl came to see me a year or two ago. She was young and beautiful, and she held the hand of her little girl. But her face was tense with horror. "Doctor, I'll do away with myself." She tried to talk calmly, but it all came out almost in a scream.

"What is the trouble?"

"It's all my fault." She clutched the little girl's hand like a drowning woman grabbing a life preserver.

"What?"

"I'll never forgive myself."

"For what? Tell me what happened."

"She's so active," she wept. "Always running around the apartment. I could never control her. She tripped and her face struck the glass table." Tears were streaming down her cheeks.

"Let me examine your little girl's face."

"I've ruined her life. She will never forgive me."

The little girl's face was bandaged. She was four years old, and frightened by her mother's crying. I removed the bandage. She had a deep, jagged wound on her right cheek near and below the lower lip. A beautiful child, with one cheek severely deformed. The wound was bleeding; I stopped the oozing and rebandaged the cheek.

"My little girl will always hate me. I should have done something to protect her."

"What?"

"I don't know, but it's my fault."

"Why? You didn't do it."

"But—will she be all right?"

"We will have to operate on her immediately."

"She'll be disfigured all her life. I'll run away. I will run away somewhere where nobody knows me. I'll. . . ."

"Stop blaming yourself," I said. "Try to calm yourself."

"They'll all hate me."

"Who?"

"My husband's parents. They never liked me anyway. They'll blame me."

I tried to soothe her, but my words had no effect. She was imprisoned in a dreadful reality, a reality-beyond-reality, in which she ended up assuming a totally unrealistic burden of guilt. The torrent of self-blame in her kept overflowing; she could not stop accusing herself.

"And my husband," she cried. "How can he ever forgive me? I have betrayed his trust."

"It was not your fault."

"It was. I'll never be able to face them. My husband will never forgive me. And neither will his parents. My darling little girl, I should have been quick enough to catch her before she struck her cheek against the glass table. Why wasn't I watching her more closely? Why wasn't I able to catch her when she tripped? I can see it all in my mind clearly; how could I be so careless as to let it happen."

My efforts to comfort the mother were useless. The picture of the accident was clearly framed in her mind; nothing could pry loose the horror, or the self-reproach.

I operated on the little girl. Then the days passed. I changed the dressing on the child's face and I tried to comfort the mother, but she clung stubbornly to visions of the accident and of her guilt.

The little girl and I would play. We didn't talk much, but we played. I would ask her her age. She would shake her head—she wouldn't tell me—I had to guess. I held up the five fingers of my right hand. She said nothing. I showed her ten fingers. She shook her head. Six fingers. No. Three fingers. No. Finally I held up four fingers and she smiled and nodded her head. We were friends.

Finally I removed the stitches. The little girl was calm enough. The mother was tense. One by one I removed the stitches. Finished.

I turned around to see an incredibly sudden transformation. Not that it surprised me; I had seen it before. The young mother's face was a study in mobility—a jet airplane whisking through blankets of fog into blinding sunshine. Her eyes sparkled for the first time in days, and big happy tears poured from them.

"You're still crying," I said.

"Oh." She sat down to wipe her eyes. "Oh."

"Is that all you can say?"

She nodded her head, and I thought to myself: tears for tragedy, tears for happiness. The same, but what a difference!

I have two reasons for telling this story:

First, I want to warn you how you can face up to reality in an obsessive, destructive way.

Second, I want to show you how, in facing up to reality, by

not minimizing the situation and by coming quickly to see me to try to remedy the damage, this woman had initiated positive action to bring about a happy ending.

Reach out to reality in a healthy way; this is the way to reach out to integrity.

7. *Industrious involvement.* Involvement in what? In making yourself the best human being that you can be. For this is worth industry, and it is also worth involvement.

The world's population continues to grow. I read, somewhere, that experts anticipate an approximate 2 percent increase in the world population each year. This deepens the already-severe problems involved in supplying adequate food for the entire population of the world. At the same time, it makes the successful application of scientific, agricultural techniques for increasing food production even more urgent than it is already. A person with integrity hates to see anyone go hungry and accepts his new role as a world citizen, trying to identify with the needs of all people in our vast world.

Still, his fundamental responsibility is to himself. His industrious involvement centers on himself. His goals: completeness, maturity, creative adjustment to life.

8. *Tenacity in thinking.* Creative thinking, that is.

As a full, complete person, you insist on your right to think for yourself. Many people let others think for them. As you move toward integrity, you refuse to allow this. This is not being arrogant; you are merely asserting your right to individuality.

Integrity, as we have said, implies wholeness and the well-integrated person sees the world from a balanced perspective. He sees that God has created millions and millions and millions of human beings, all unique individuals, each owing it to himself to nurture the roots of his uniqueness. In an age of conformity, he insists on his right to think for himself.

9. *Yearning for emotional nourishment.* Finally, in spelling out the components of integrity, we come to "yearning for emotional nourishment." While you may aspire to be honest, principled, and complete, you need a feeling that you can reach out to feed yourself, in abundance, to feel the full satisfaction of well-balanced integrity.

There is an old Saxon toast. The devoted lover, letting the sharp edge of his poniard lightly cut his forehead, dribbled his blood into his wine cup, and then drank the mixture in honor of his beloved. Physical nourishment? Emotional nourishment? I know it's too strong for my tastes.

But this custom, centuries old, and now a barbarous anachronism, seems to me symbolic of the human yearning for an overpowering nourishment process which seems basically of an emotional nature.

If you don't eat, you don't live but in our technological age, eating is an emotional process. To be a full person, you need "food" for thought, "substance" in your relationships, a "wholesome" motivation.

Integrity and Self-Respect

Reread this spelling-out exercise whenever you have some spare time.

Integrity is a key component of self-respect; because the individual with integrity is balanced, thoughtful, and responsible. He gives other people a sense of security; surely he must give himself as much.

"Integrity," you may say. "Who has time for it?"

You.

"Me?" I'm so busy most of the time I could hardly tell you my name."

But you have to find time to develop integrity. Just as you must find time to build in yourself such fine qualities as sincerity, understanding, the capacity for active forgiveness, and creative mirror-watching. What are you without integrity? A hunted animal? A clock watcher? A robot?

"Words," you may say. "More words. They don't mean anything. Integrity. One more word."

You think so? Then you are wrong. In my theory of creative psycho-cybernetics, we move from words, to images, to action. To see how, turn to Chapter 15, "Goal-Builders," in which we will work on practical exercises for self-respect.

But for now take time to develop your capacity for integrity. Do you have time to cook supper? Or wash your car? Or go to the beauty parlor? Or the barbershop? Do you have time to pay your income tax? Or make a bank deposit? Or to open your mail and read it? Then you can find time to work with yourself on your most important emotional level, building a sense of wholeness, of rational perspective, of sincere trustworthiness.

Integrity. If you have it, how can you not respect yourself?

In a dinner, dessert and coffee follow the main course. In your emotional life, self-respect follows integrity.

Our search for self-respect is no wild, far-out scramble. We build qualities and capacities; we focus on positive concepts and images. We go from integrity to self-respect.

CHAPTER 14

Survival with Self-Respect

SURVIVAL is of necessity a basic human goal. It is a timeless goal. Down through the centuries—from the flowering of Greek culture to the savagery of the Crusades to the sterility of the Middle Ages to today's dynamic, ever-changing world —man has struggled for survival.

Life, a precious gift. We fight to preserve it. We fight with all our resources.

Still, we seek more than mere physical survival—and that is the theme of this book and, indeed, of creative psycho-cybernetics. We seek a constructive form of survival. We seek a survival that is meaningful and honorable. We seek a live, give-and-take form of survival.

Physical survival is in itself a fine, instinctive aim. That many people are successful in living to an advanced age is obvious; social security statistics will illustrate this, I am sure.

But we seek more than this: We seek a qualitative survival. A survival with self-respect.

This is no small accomplishment; you cannot reach it overnight or by pushing a button or mouthing a few magic words. It takes hard work and purposeful thinking-imaging which surfaces into positive action.

Where do you start?

By understanding, to begin with, that survival with self-respect is a human possibility. That you can make it a lifetime goal and still cling to sanity. That you can make it a lifetime goal and rise above sanity to full living.

This is an age of confusion and cynicism, and millions upon millions of people have come to doubt themselves. It is one of our greatest tragedies that so many people today feel disillusionment, not hope; humiliation, not pride in self; debasement, not self-respect.

When you set a goal, you must believe in that goal. Therefore, if survival with self-respect is your goal, you must believe you can achieve it. When you have your goal in focus, only then can you move toward it effectively.

In the early 1900s, man was still struggling to fly; and it was a struggle. Many were skeptics, and felt that man would never fly. Samuel Langley was one of the world's most eminent scientists. The newspapers gave enormous publicity to his flying machine. When it failed, skepticism about man's possibility of flying rose to a new high. This lent still greater stature to the achievement of the Wright brothers. Where others doubted, they believed; and they backed their belief with intensity. In their experiments—both near home and at Kitty Hawk, North Carolina—the Wright brothers backed belief with a creative, realistic approach. When they failed, they analyzed the reasons for their failures. As no one before them, they applied themselves with a keen, excited concentration to each problem. They solved the problem of flight control and, early in the twentieth century, they made the skeptics blink their eyes and reassemble their thoughts.

What about you? You, too, can fly. Don't let the skeptics tell you it's impossible.

You fly when you set survival with self-respect as your goal, and you move toward it.

You fly when you believe in such a meaningful goal and believe you deserve such an attainment.

You fly when you resolve to rise above your failures, your dissociations and your disappointments to reclaim the better side of yourself, to stake a claim in that better side—a Columbus courageous in your powers.

Here is my main point: You have this better side. No matter who you are, no matter how difficult your life, no matter how many your frustrations and your failures, you have this better side.

Reclaim this better side. I congratulate you on your physical survival, but take one giant step farther and work toward a survival with self-respect.

The pace of the world moves forward. Yesterday, the Wright brothers pioneered flight. Today, the astronauts pioneer the moon.

Not too long ago astronauts Armstrong and Aldrin descended onto the moon—on the right side of the moon—and Neil Armstrong stepped out of his landing craft to make history.

Then it was the turn of astronauts Conrad and Bean. Another fantastic technological achievement. There they were, Conrad and Bean, landing near a crater on the Ocean of Storms—also on the right side of the moon.

Once people had said it could never be done. But, backed

by billions of dollars and hundreds of thousands of people, they did it.

What an achievement!

From science fiction to reality: Men on the moon—on the right side of the moon.

But let us hypothesize. Let us assume a miscalculation, a failure in communication, a misdirection. Our astronauts, through error, might have landed on the dark side of the moon, there to be lost forever on that bleak and barren landscape—on the wrong side of the moon.

But how does this apply to you?

You, too, have two sides: a side that leads you to failure and frustration, and a side that leads you to success and confidence. Every day, through torturing themselves over their errors, their guilts, their misfortunes, millions of people step out into the world on the wrong side of themselves, the one that leads to failure: the wrong side. You may survive the misery, in the physical sense, but where is your self-respect?

Whizzing around the earth at unbelievable speeds, our astronauts see an earth which is half the time in shadow, half the time in sunlight.

And you? You must become a psycho-cybernaut, steering through your mind toward inspiring goals, weaving through your negative feelings toward the person you want to be, jet-propelling yourself through shadow into sunlight. Your instrument panel is not complicated, and you do not have to be a trained technician. All you need is to win that crucial battle in your mind, between your negative and positive forces, reactivating your success mechanism, not your failure mechanism, fighting through to your better side, then carrying your emotional triumph out into the world of action.

Psycho-cybernauts, too, are creative and courageous adventurers. They venture into a land that many people fear—the land of inner space. They seek control over this area in themselves, positive and constructive control of an area which many people mark as "off limits."

Psycho-cybernauts, brave and hardy, seek the raw materials in themselves with which to manufacture that champagne of the emotional life—self-respect.

They steer themselves toward the best kind of life—survival with self-respect.

No Survival (without Self-Respect)

Now let us examine the components of No Survival, by spelling them out:

1. Negative feelings.
2. Oppression.

3. Separation.
4. Unacceptableness.
5. Resistance to living
6. Vacillation.
7. Indifference.
8. Vulnerability.
9. Absenteeism.
10. Lamenting yesterday.

The airplane that buckles before it gets off the ground. The flight to the wrong side of the moon. The earth in shadow. NO SURVIVAL.

1. Negative feelings. You can't get off the ground. Your negative feelings are weighing you down. You can't forget your past mistakes. You can't forgive yourself. You move forward with turtle speed. You go on living, but your days are agonizing.

2. *Oppression.* You are a living embodiment of the failure mechanism. Your life is a morass of failure. Fearfully you walk around, lonely and uncertain, choking with resentment, empty and despairing. You go through the motions of living while under the cloud of a sense of inferiority, reacting to your chronic frustrations with mischanneled aggressiveness, antagonizing others, and humilating yourself.

You go on living? Fine. But what is the caliber of your survival? Do you survive with self-respect? No, you oppress yourself with failure.

3. *Separation.* You separate yourself from more than the mainstream of people. You estrange yourself from yourself. You deny the worth of your self-image.

You separate yourself from an appreciation of your assets, of your capacities, of your possibilities.

You separate yourself from your feelings of success and from your smile of confidence.

Yielding to futility, you drift into nothingness as a status quo.

You discontinue your dialogue for your emotional improvement, and the resulting monologue signifies that you are growing older, not wiser.

4. *Unacceptableness.* Who is unacceptable? You are. In whose opinion? In your own.

This is an intolerable state. You blow the whistle on your self-esteem. You call yourself out on strikes. You mark the papers and grade yourself "F." You sentence yourself to life imprisonment.

You are referee, umpire, teacher, judge. You will not give yourself the same justice you give others. You refuse to accept yourself and, with your acceptance, give yourself a chance to give your life meaning.

5. Resistance to living. Too many of us chip away segments of our self-respect every day because we resist living in the present and bury our creativity in the quicksand of the past. But coddling our regrets leads us into cycles of defeat and therefore such resistance to living in the present leads us into a life of boredom and, blinding ourselves to possibility, into crosscurrents of cynicism.

6. Vacillation. When you vacillate, again and again, you deny yourself the world of action.

If, through vacillation, you block off your goals, inhibiting yourself from action, you will find yourself slowly drowning. In a way it is a safe form of drowning since your body survives.

But, by playing it so safe that you continually vacillate, by never taking a chance, you drown emotionally. You go under. You refuse to surface for action. You deny yourself artificial respiration. Your body lives on, but your emotional self is drowning, and you do not hear your own cry for help.

7. Indifference. This is, beyond doubt, one of the most horrifying words in the English language. To feel indifference when one breathes life—what an inhuman fate! To feel indifference when one enjoys God's great gift of life, this is most pitiful.

To survive the years, to win out in the great battle for

time, what a feast for the human being! To squander this time, feeling indifference and emptiness, what waste! It is terrifying to spend a life in the shadows when there is sunshine. Real living, with real self-respect, involves human feeling—not indifference.

8. *Vulnerability.* Vulnerability is an integral component of nonsurvival. You leave yourself vulnerable to defeat when you fail to support yourself emotionally. In defeat, you vanish from yourself, and from your world. You become one of those invisible people of modern times, one of the millions of visible/invisible people who survive without a sense of real participation.

Feeling vulnerable, you succumb to dizziness when you try to move toward your goals. This is emotional dizziness. You are seasick, carsick, planesick—without ever going out to meet the world.

9. *Absenteeism.* A great problem in industry is absenteeism. Millions and millions of dollars lost. Production schedules disrupted. Corporations hold meetings to deal with the problem.

But we refer here to your greatest industry—YOU—and your problem with your own absenteeism. When you are not on the job, helping yourself, strengthening your self-image, you lessen your productivity and find yourself wallowing in a form of survival that lacks any real meaning.

10. *Lamenting yesterday.* This is a sad song. Don't sing it again, Sam—or Mabel—or Harry—or Joan. Don't sing it again, this lament of yesteryear. It is not harmonious. The melody is discordant. Further, it is inappropriate to the occasion. Pull out another sheet of music. That's it! Sing a song of today!

The Tall Midget and the "Little Self"

Living with or without self-respect, that is the question. We have spelled out NO SURVIVAL. Now SURVIVAL.

But first, two stories: One, about a midget who lived with a full sense of self-respect. The other, about a normal-sized woman who felt chronically humiliated and who thought of herself as a "little self."

I met the midget in Toronto, Canada. It was a few weeks before Christmas and I sat in the lobby of a Toronto hotel. It was a huge lobby and some people were putting up a Christmas tree. I was waiting to lunch with a friend and had nothing to do, so I watched them setting up the Christmas tree—a huge tree, twenty-six feet high, someone said—installing lights and decorations. I watched the Christmas tree glitter awhile and then my attention strayed to a tiny bellhop whose job it was to call out people's names into a microphone, or loud-speaker system, or whatever. His appearance was striking. Apparently in his forties, he seemed little more than three feet tall. He was engaged in his work, paging people, then smiling and joking with co-workers in a most amiable way. I could not take my eyes off him for, tiny as he was, he breathed forth a feeling of confidence and good nature.

He left his post for a minute and walked over to look at the tree. There he stood, under the tree, looking almost like a happy little doll, a present to go with the tree, talking to the men putting it up, laughing with them, a talking, laughing doll.

Then back to his post, calling out people's names in clear, friendly tones, functioning smoothly in his job—calm, mature, full of self-assurance.

Maybe he was physically a midget, I told myself, but his

self-image is as tall as that twenty-six-foot Christmas tree. Growing up deformed, he had outgrown his physical defects and reached the full stature of his self-respect.

When I returned home to New York City, a girl in her twenties came to see me—a normal-sized girl, pretty too—and I found myself thinking of the emotionally tall midget and contrasting him to this attractive, physically normal girl with a tiny self-image.

"My 'little self' is killing me," she said.

"What?"

"My 'little self.' It's killing me."

"I hadn't noticed," I remarked.

"Noticed what?"

"Your 'little self.' What about your 'big self'?"

"I don't have a 'big self.' I'm not much. I don't kid myself. My 'little self,' it's killing me."

She came from out of town, she told me, Her father and mother were always bickering. One argument after another, that was her home life. She thought of herself as a "little self."

She wanted to be an actress, but found she was blocking herself from her goal with constant feelings of inferiority. Her mother had also wanted to be an actress when she was younger but had failed. Resenting the child, her mother had ridiculed her for her ambition: How could the daughter make a success as an actress when she, her mother, had failed! What was the daughter, anyway? Only a "little self."

She sat across from me, this attractive, intelligent girl in her twenties. "How can I become an actress? My 'little self' is killing me."

"You have a 'big self,'" I told her. "And maybe you can make a go of an acting career. Let me tell you a story. There was this fine teacher of drama and she had this young girl pupil, a marvelous actress, who pitched into every new role with such vigor that she was successful in all of them."

"I wish I was half as good."

"She hated herself so much in real life that she loved to pretend she was someone else and she played fictitious roles with great zest. The teacher then asked her to enact the role of her better self in real life. She did, and became a better human being as well as a fine actress. You try this, won't you? Develop your skills as an actress, escaping from your self to become someone else; then, in real life, work at playing the role of the better you. Maybe you'll be a better actress and a better human being, maybe you'll find you're your 'big self,' and maybe you'll forget about your 'little self' and start living."

Eight months later she came to see me. She was radiant. She had finally found her better self—her "big self," and she had landed a job in the cast of an off-Broadway musical.

We have spelled out NO SURVIVAL; now let us spell out SURVIVAL.

Survival

First, our list:

1. *S*ense of forward movement.
2. *U*pgrading.
3. *R*elaxed attitude.
4. *V*itality.
5. *I*maginative power.
6. *V*alues.
7. *A*spiration for happiness.
8. *L*iving now.

That's our chart for survival with self-respect. Now let us work on it.

1. Sense of forward movement. You move forward toward your goals. You will not find meaning in your life through adding up your birthdays or sitting around worrying about the world's dangers. Set your goals; then move out toward them. This is your first step toward a form of survival with real meaning.

2. Upgrading. Many people spend their lives downgrading themselves, heaping contempt upon themselves, then accepting or resenting the humiliations that other people push upon them.

Stop downgrading yourself and making excuses for yourself. Upgrade yourself. See your past successes, and feel them. Give yourself credit for your accomplishments. Stand up to pressure and to fear. Re-evaluate your self-image, and re-evaluate with kind eyes, befriending yourself and giving yourself the benefit of the doubt.

3. Relaxed attitude. Forgive—yourself, first of all, then others too. By doing this you can build a relaxed attitude that will help you survive with a good feeling about yourself.

Forgive completely—not on the installment plan. A little here, a little there is not good enough.

Pick up your eraser and wipe the chalk off the blackboard, all the chalk. Leave a clean slate with no grudges, no lifelong condemnations, and no obsession with past grievances. Wipe the slate absolutely clean.

Then approach yourself and your world with a relaxed attitude, which will smooth your path to living with self-respect.

4. Vitality. Concentrate on what you're doing. Act with intensity. When you have formulated a goal, release your full vitality in your attempt to achieve that goal. Halfhearted actions seldom succeed. Put your full energy into cementing your goals.

Remember this: A near-success is a failure. You must follow through to your goals with all the vitality that is in you.

5. Imaginative power. Used creatively, this means survival with dignity.

You use this enormous power creatively when you use your imagination for building a positive image of yourself, for seeing again and again your past successes, for envisioning goals that inspire you and foreseeing tactics to move you toward your goals.

Stop using your imagination for storing the memory of all your past mistakes and miseries. Use it to build, not destroy, yourself.

6. Values. What is there in life you need, and what is excess baggage? What is valuable, and what is irrelevant? You must adjust your values sensibly so you can stress helpful focuses in your search for dignified living.

You must learn to value solid human values: constructive motivation, compassion, forgiveness, and self-fulfillment, a strong self-image, and a feeling that you are a winner as one of life's money players.

You build survival for self-respect on the bedrock of strong values.

7. Aspiration for happiness. Your aspiration is universal. You aspire to help yourself to happiness, and you aspire to help others too. You fight to bolster your courage in withstanding life's pressures; you try to give your courage to others.

Don't replay that old record of frustration. It is a long-playing record; sometimes it never stops. Play a new record:

of aspiration for happiness as a fundamental goal. Place it on the turntable now.

This is a rough, competitive world and you cannot always live up to your ideals; but try—at least, try—to act in a brotherly way toward other people whenever this is practical. Some will reciprocate, and your aspirations for happiness will reap rich harvests.

8. Living now. Now that you have my ideas for survival with self-respect, I must ask you when you will go to work on them. Did I hear you say "Tomorrow"?

Please. I can't stand that word. I've heard it for over sixty-five years now, and I can't stand it, because I know it really means "never."

Live now. Today. You survive with respect when you live today and forget the fantasy of "tomorrow."

Live today. Reactivating your success mechanism, channel your sense of direction toward positive and attainable goals, accept yourself for what you are, and work on creative attitudes toward yourself and other people. Survival with self-respect means *SUCCESS,* and success begins today.

The Anatomy of Self-Respect

In these first fourteen chapters, we have dissected the anatomy of self-respect.

We have discussed the nature and importance of self-respect. We have analyzed the role of understanding and of active sincerity, in the attainment of human dignity. After treating, at length, some of the roadblocks to self-respect, we have analyzed the proper application of active forgiveness and the constructive use of mirror watching, among other factors, in the anatomy of self-respect.

We have stressed the active approach—thoughtful imaging which leads to constructive action. This active approach is basic to my theory of creative psycho-cybernetics.

To illustrate my point, I have told a series of stories about myself, my friends, and people who have come to talk to me, while preserving the anonymity of people where there is confidential material.

Now, we will sing about survival with self-respect. Why "sing"? Well, isn't this something to "sing" about? To many people, life is arithmetical. You live to the age of fifty or sixty or sixty-five or—but let's stop here. Because at sixty-five most people believe in survival—period. Most people abandon all creative living and, with it, a good measure of self-respect as they retreat into an absurd state known as retirement.

Survival with self-respect. How that reminds me of the great cellist Pablo Casals! This wonderful man seems to get younger all the time. Last I heard he was ninety-two and still going strong.

Casals, exiled from his native Spain for almost half his life, is a man of courage and moral principle, a brave fighter for just causes. He spent years fighting to bring good music at reasonable prices to the common people of Spain. Having recovered from a heart attack, he went right on working, participating in his music festivals, and embarking on a peace crusade.

Casals is a young man in his nineties, surviving the many years with an enormous amount of self-respect: Truly he is an inspiration to all of us.

Casals has always been too in love with life to worry himself about arithmetic, too enthused about his great lifelong goal of giving to people through music, to let chronological numbers eat into his sense of constructive participation in the world.

When this book comes out, will he still be alive? No matter, he will long be an inspiration.

Survival with self-respect. This finishes our analysis of the anatomy of self-respect, except for a short physical examination.

When you go to see a doctor, he examines you. Perhaps your heart, lungs and blood pressure are normal, but then he puts you under a special kind of microscope. A worried look on his face now. "Your self-respect," he tells you. "It has vanished. Physically you're okay, but emotionally—I'm sorry to tell you this—you are invisible."

You leap to your feet. "What's the prognosis, doctor?"

"*No survival.*"

"What can you do for me, doctor?"

"The point is, what can you do for yourself?"

"I don't understand."

"You have lost faith in yourself. Your blood pressure is fine and all the tests check out fine, but emotionally you are invisible. You have lost self-respect. But I can't help you regain it. You have to do this for yourself."

A horrifying fantasy? True.

But my point is this: You must assume responsibility in this great search for your self-respect.

Ask yourself this: Would you fail this examination? Would your self-respect be invisible?

If so, your search is not over.

Go on to the final chapter, "Goal Builders," in which we will work to turn theory into reality, with a series of exercises I've designed to help you find your full self-respect as a human being.

CHAPTER 15

Goal Builders

Now we have reached the end of our voyage of discovery. We have completed our search; now we have found our self-respect.

Or have we?

We have launched a major drive toward self-respect. We have analyzed its components; we have focused on its importance; we have shuffled our values and rearranged our priorities, but what about self-respect? We have concentrated our energies to seek out a direction of thinking that will bring us self-respect, a utilization of our imagination that will bring us self-respect, a constructive orientation toward the world and our human brothers and sisters that will bring us self-respect.

Still, we have not concluded our search. And perhaps we never will. For the search for self-respect is a lifetime job. When you feel self-respect, you still seek more, and when you find more, you keep your momentum alive and give your self-respect to others. You share. You give. This is the creative spirit that enriches you as you devote yourself to enriching others.

In this final chapter, we end our voyage, but for a while only. For, just as we like to save our money week after week and month after month and year after year, we must also attune ourselves to the importance of continually building our sense of self-respect. Self-respect is even more basic than money. If you are frugal, you can survive with just a little money and live a good life—but life without self-respect is a wasteland.

I call this concluding chapter "Goal Builders" because we will now focus, one by one, on the goals we have outlined in the previous chapters of this book. For each chapter, I have devised an exercise to help you take firm hold of the goal that is stressed. I feel that this is the key to this book. Because my words will not help you enough if they remain passively on the paper; you can make them come alive if you use them to strengthen your emotional muscles by working on these exercises. This is my concept of creative psycho-cybernetics. You move from constructive thinking to constructive imaging, and on to constructive action—goal builders for self-respect.

This is a fourteen-week building-up process. Here is how you go about it. Give each goal builder one full week: work on it for six days, then take a day off. You are a creative mirror watcher for self-respect. Six days a week—for fourteen weeks—you build. Fourteen chapters, fourteen goal builders. Your first goal builder is self-respect itself. Your other goal builders are the components of self-respect. In Chapter 9, I stress the enormous impact of creative mirror watching. Use it as you work on these exercises, moving from goal builder to goal builder. One full week on each: six days of application, then one day of rest. They add up to what we're starting with—self-respect.

Goal Builder 1. *Self-Respect*

Do you feel guilty and keep blaming yourself for all your past mistakes, downgrading yourself as a human being? Help yourself; try this.

Close your eyes; sit down in a quiet place; imagine that you are a convicted criminal living behind bars. You've seen your share of prison movies. See them again in your mind, but you're one of the actors. You're playing one of the heavies; you are ruthless, embittered, totally antisocial. You are unmanageable. You shake the bars of your prison cell, screaming curses at the guards. Eating with the other prisoners, you beat your plate with your fork, trying to stir up an inmate riot. You never talk; you only snarl. You are so mean you make James Cagney's old gangster roles seem angelic. The warden, a kindly man, comes to see if he can reform you; you try to attack him and the guards wrestle you to the ground howling threats of revenge.

Now, back to reality. Are you really such a terrible fellow that you should deny yourself self-respect, feeling guilty about everything? Why?

This criminal you imagined you were, he was guilty of all kinds of irresponsible, antisocial behavior. But you? You were just imagining you were like this. Are you like this—in reality? Of course not.

Then why do you keep treating yourself as if you were loathsome, distorted, guilty? You do your best; you try to be a constructive human being. Give yourself credit for this. Stop convicting yourself of crimes. Stop putting yourself behind bars. Feed yourself self-respect. Remind yourself of your virtues once in a while.

But go beyond this. Walk over to a mirror in your home and look at yourself. Ask yourself: "Do I see a distorted version of myself? Do I fail to see my value? Do I shortchange myself and deprive myself of self-respect?"

Take out a lipstick or an erasable pencil and in large capital letters—don't be afraid—write on the mirror SELF-RE-SPECT. You can erase it later. Meanwhile, leave the word on the mirror, look at it and at yourself.

Say to your image in the mirror: "Today I will try to respect myself. I deserve to respect myself."

Back to my prison movie, let me, in fairness, add a footnote because in lecturing around the country I have talked to many convicted criminals, inmates of our penitentiaries: I suggest this Hollywood-type criminal image to help you feel how ludicrous it is to obsess yourself with guilt and deny yourself self-respect, but this image is largely a distortion. I have talked to men in prison who had fine, constructive attitudes. Some criminals have paid for their offenses and want another chance to build wholesome lives; they deserve our compassion. Self-respect is their right too.

Goal Builder 2. *Understanding*

Walking down the street, you look at all the people. You have walked down this street before—in New York or St. Louis or wherever—but this time you get more than physical exercise. You get mental exercise too. For you are trying to focus on an understanding that has often eluded you: the understanding that you have the right to live happily, pleasurably, and with self-respect. This is a basic understanding.

You glance at the people you pass on the sidewalk. They are so alike—yet so different. You are concentrating on observing one thing that differentiates them: their feeling that they have rights or their conviction that they have no rights.

With this in mind, you study the people you meet. You look at this person or that person and you ask yourself, "Does he (or she) believe he has the right to be happy?"

In many cases, on such superficial consideration, you can come to no sure conclusion. Some people may be in "up" moods while others are in "down" moods. Many successfully hide their feelings. Others register neutral or mixed impressions on the most careful observer.

But some people, you will see, slouch and stumble as they walk, avert their eyes in an excess of timidity, seem empty of any feeling but fear. A percentage of these people may be only temporarily "down," but it is a fair assumption that many habitually short-change themselves, refusing to understand that they are as good as other people and have the right to a life of happiness and self-respect.

You see other people who, without swaggering or stepping on other people's toes or overcompensating, walk proud and erect, looking others in the eye with friendliness and a smile of confidence. Again, you cannot be sure, but it is a fair bet that many of these people give themselves rights and feel they are deserving.

You have finished your walk; you walk back home. Now go to your mirror; you will use this mirror again and again. Once again, take out an erasable pencil or lipstick and write on the mirror—in capital letters, bold and clear, UNDERSTANDING.

Say to yourself, looking at yourself in the mirror, "I have seen people who feel they have rights and other people who feel they have no rights (and also, of course, people with mixed feelings). But how about me? Do I have rights? Yes. Yes, I do."

Erase the word UNDERSTANDING from your mirror but keep alive in you the feeling that you do have rights. Subject to the restrictions of our civilized laws, you have the right to enjoy life and to respect yourself and to make each day a good day.

Goal Builder 3. *Sincerity*

People disagree on many issues, but most people would agree to this statement: Sincerity is not a quality many human beings possess these days.

This is tragic.

Sincerity is a fine trait. The sincere person gives substance to human relations. He enriches himself and he also enriches others.

But sincerity requires confidence; it requires enough belief in yourself so that you can face up to reality without evasion.

So the question is: How do you build confidence in yourself?

This is no overnight proposition, but I think this exercise will help:

Once again, seat yourself in a quiet room and close your eyes and let your imagination go to work for you. This time you will visit an amusement park in your mind. See it—the merry-go-round, the barkers, the roller coaster and all the other "thrill" rides.

You walk by a crowd of giggling girls and then a young couple, arm in arm, and a man in work clothes munching a hot dog.

Your destination? The "fun" mirrors.

Remember them? The mirrors that distort your form so ludicrously that you stare at yourself in amazement? Short? Tall? Thin as a pencil? Bulging with fat? People come to laugh and laugh as they see themselves in the "fun" mirrors; their reflections are too ridiculous to threaten them.

In your mind, now, you see yourself in one of these distorting mirrors. How ridiculous you look! How can anyone take you seriously?

Back to reality now; open your eyes. Walk over to your mirror; write the word SINCERITY on it.

The grotesque physical distortions of the "fun" mirror did not disturb you. But how about your real image?

Look at yourself in the mirror; and ask yourself this: "Do I emotionally distort myself, taking away my confidence and my capacity for sincerity? Do I see myself as a distorted person when other people disapprove of me? Do I feel I am ridiculous when I make a minor mistake?"

If you do, remember the distortions of the "fun" mirrors.

"They are ridiculous," you say?

True—but when you distort yourself emotionally, taking away your feeling of confidence and your capacity for sincerity, is this not equally ridiculous?

I feel strongly that this amusement park "fun" mirror exercise can help many people. If you can see that when you torture yourself for your imperfections you are distorting your self-image "fun-mirror" style, and if you can use this comparison visually to laugh at yourself as you would do at an amusement park, then perhaps you can begin to stop yourself.

With practice you will be able to do this with more and more ease until you can finally see yourself with a smile of confidence. Then you will be able to practice sincerity in your relations with other people.

Goal Builder 4. *Defeating Uncertainty*

Once again, the only tools you need are a place to seat yourself, some quiet, and your imagination.

You close your eyes and see a motion picture.

It is World War II. You are a Marine in the Pacific. You have landed with your buddies on a heavily-fortified island. The first wave of attackers was wiped out by the enemy soldiers defending the island. You are fortunate; you were in the second wave and you survived. You and your fellows advanced into the jungle—perhaps half a mile. Now, you are in darkness. Suddenly you realize you haven't seen one of your buddies in fifteen minutes. You can't see anyone. You can't shout; the enemy might be behind the next tree. You are cut off—perhaps for the whole night. Will you still be alive the next morning?

Scared? Sure you are; I am too.

My point?

That your life, no matter how filled with uncertainties, could be worse. The nightmare you just lived through in your mind, suppose this was your reality?

If you find this revisualization of World War II in the Pacific too unsettling to bear, see any other terrifying experience in your mind—another war, an automobile accident, your house on fire. My point is that you must learn to deal with life's uncertainties in order to feel a real sense of self-respect; seeing such a terrifying "motion picture" may (assuming your reality is not so monstrous) help you to return with relief to your own life situation.

It may make your problems seem smaller by comparison and therefore more manageable. Thus it may help you to stand firm and cope with them instead of running away from life into fantasy.

Go back to your mirror once more. Walk over and with erasable pencil or lipstick write DEFEAT UNCERTAINTY. That is your goal.

Look in the mirror and say to yourself, "I know that life is uncertain, but I will try to face my problems and troubles as best as I can and not run to hide at the first sign of danger. When situations test my patience and courage, I will try to stand up to them."

It is basic to my theory of creative psycho-cybernetics that you do more than theorize about handling uncertainty. When it is practicable, translate theory into action, moving toward your objective with wisdom and determination—in spite of uncertainties.

Difficult? Yes. But you will respect yourself for your courage, and this is most rewarding.

Goal Builder 5. *Overcoming Resentment*

Resentment is a way of life with too many people. How do you overcome it?

One helpful technique is to work at handling your anxieties more rationally, because anxieties lead to resentment.

Today you are worried about this or that. How do you manage your fears?

Think back to last week. What were your anxieties then? Write them down.

Think back to last month. What were your anxieties then? Write them down.

Can you remember what you were worried about a year ago? If you can, write these fears down.

Now take your list and study it. Check out your anxieties. Was this one realistic? Did it make any sense? Or that one?

Many people worry about things that never happen and there is a splendid chance that, as you check out your list of anxieties, you will find that many—perhaps most—of your worries were unrealistic.

If you discover this, hopefully this insight into your over-reactions will help you deal more realistically with your present fears and thus reduce your resentment. And, with less resentment, you move toward richer living and heightened self-respect.

Now, to the mirror, and write: OVERCOME RESENT-MENT.

Tell yourself that you will overcome your resentment. Say to yourself, "I will try to overcome my resentment every way I can. I will try to reduce my anxieties. I will set constructive goals. I want self-respect."

Goal Builder 6. *Getting Rid of Emptiness*

The empty person lacks goals. His emptiness is linked with his indifference about the events of his day.

If you feel this apathy, rise above it. To the mirror, and write NO EMPTINESS. Then work to make these words meaningful.

Look at yourself in the mirror and tell yourself, "I will make my life mean something. Time is my treasure and I will not waste it. I will set goals to give meaning to my precious days."

Then take a pad and pencil. Think of a goal and write it down. Weigh it. Is it your goal? Does it mean something to you? Can you achieve this goal? Do you have a fighting chance, at least? Keep writing and thinking until you have found goals to give purpose to your life.

Or perhaps you may prefer putting away pad and pencil in a drawer, seating yourself comfortably, closing your eyes, and once more using your imagination, searching your mind for meaningful goals, inventorying your past experiences and visualizing current possibilities.

These are two techniques for formulating goals; perhaps you can devise a technique that works better for you than these would. The main point is that you must orient yourself toward goals and self-respect and full living and away from an inner sense of emptiness that is a repudiation of your life force.

Goal Builder 7. *Opportunity*

Recently, a friend of mine with small children showed me a wonderful children's book by Dr. Seuss called *Green Eggs and Ham* (Random House, 1960). It is a most comic book. There is a small, nondescript, mischievous-looking animal trying to induce a larger, more grouchy, equally nondescript animal to eat green eggs and ham on a platter. This small animal—Sam-I-am—keeps prodding the big grouch to try the green eggs and ham. He is a high-pressure salesman without peer. He follows the other animal over hill and dale, cross-country, and finally under water in his singleminded determination to get him to eat the green eggs and ham. The big animal keeps refusing to try the dish, insisting he does not like it, thwarting Sam-I-am in a Keystone-Cops-type chase; under no circumstances, he insists, will he eat green eggs and ham.

But finally he gives in; and, to his surprise, he finds that he likes green eggs and ham. He likes them very much.

Why do I tell this story?

Certainly not to commend to you green eggs and ham. To tell you the truth, even the words make me feel mildly nauseated.

For me, this story has an allegorical meaning. It suggests that people shy away from new experiences, run away from experimentation, fail to explore life's many opportunities for satisfaction. Many people will explore new avenues of opportunity only under compulsion.

Do you welcome constructive opportunities, or is your fear stronger than your sense of creative adventure?

When you wake up in the morning, walk over to your mirror and write: OPPORTUNITY.

Then ask yourself, "What opportunities await me today? How can I make today a good day?"

Close your eyes; see them in your mind. Take out paper and pencil and write them down. Then plot your course of action.

Back to Goal Builder 2, *Understanding,* remember that you have the right to move toward opportunity—without trampling on others' rights—and to feel happy.

Goal Builder 8. *Forgiveness*

On the mirror draw an arrow and say: "From forgiveness to self-respect." For this relationship is fundamental. If you do not forgive yourself for your limitations and your failures, you cannot give yourself the wonderful gift of self-respect.

Do you find that you cannot stop blaming yourself? You cannot stop the flow of self-condemnation? Your self-critical thoughts overwhelm you?

Try another movie in your imagination. This time picture a "torture scene"—a gruesome, horrifying scene of physical torture. The "enemy" holds you prisoner and tries to force secrets from you. "So you won't talk, eh? We'll see about that."

Is this too horrifying? I agree. Do you want me to stop? Then I will.

But what about your own cruel self-torture? Is this not equally horrifying? Equally inhuman? Can any "enemy" with whatever ruthless refinements of physical torture inflict more damage on you than you can inflict on yourself with your ceaseless critical self-mutilation?

On your mirror, erase the arrow and write FORGIVE-NESS. Say, "I will try to forgive myself. I will try to forgive others. We are all human and imperfect."

The next step is self-respect.

Goal Builder 9. *Creative Mirror Watching*

I decided to insert the word "creative" because if you misapply mirror watching, you can make it an exercise in narcissism, superficial apathy, or critical self-destruction. Your aim is seeing behind your face to the mature, dynamic, and compassionate person you want to become.

Step to the mirror. Don't panic; it's only you.

Look at yourself this time in absolute honesty, evaluating

yourself. No, don't run away. The mirror won't break; don't let it break you.

About face! You weren't in the army? All right, then, just turn around. And walk away.

Now think. The sight of your face, did it evoke a torrent of critical thoughts? If it did, ask yourself this: Do you feel this hostile when you see the face of a friend when he comes into your home or when you enter his home?

Back to the mirror.

But this time look at yourself as you would look at a friend. Close your eyes for a moment and see the face of this good friend; select a specific friend and see his or her face. You feel a positive feeling at the recollection? All right; now open your eyes. That's you in the mirror. Write FRIEND on the mirror; that's you.

Say to yourself, "I will be a friend to myself. I will look at myself with kind eyes. With compassion for my imperfections. With appreciation of my capacities."

Tackling Goal Builder 3, *Sincerity,* we emphasized the physical distortion of amusement park "funhouse" mirrors, and compared the harmless and amusing effect of these images to the crippling impact of emotional distortion. Be creative: Stop distorting your self-image and take a giant stride toward self-respect.

Goal Builder 10. *Tearing Down Prison Walls*

You feel imprisoned in your own home or at a party? Even walking down the street, swinging freely you feel unreasonably trapped? Civilization imposes limits on what people can do, but perhaps you overinhibit yourself beyond these limits. Tear down those prison walls!

I think this exercise will help you because overinhibition usually stems from lack of confidence, which comes from chronic failure.

Once again, seat yourself comfortably, quietly, and close your eyes. Imagine you are playing baseball. It is your turn at bat. You swing a few bats, to warm up, hand one to the bat boy, and stride to home plate. You assume your stance, crouching slightly and facing the pitcher. You want to get a hit.

But you know from past experience that this is a tough pitcher. His fastball is overpowering; his curve is sharp; his change of pace throws you off balance. His control is his strongest asset; he keeps the ball away from you and nicks the corner of the plate. In the past, he has struck you out repeatedly. You feel defeated the moment you look at him. What can you do?

Ah, you remember something. In the past, you came to the plate determined to hit home runs. But this pitcher is too tough for you to hit for home runs. Trying to belt home runs and striking out, again and again, you tie yourself up in knots of frustration. Your goal is unrealistic.

You can and must realign your goal. You can stop trying for the skyrocketing home run blast and aim at meeting the ball squarely. A line drive between the infielders is good for a solid single, and that will do fine.

So you shorten up your grip on the bat, eliminate the unrealistic fantasy that you are Babe Ruth, and aim at punching out a single. This pitcher may still get you out—he is tough—but you will get your share of hits now that your goal is realistic.

Along with your share of hits, you will gain confidence.

With confidence, you need no longer imprison yourself so cruelly.

On your mirror write: PRISON. Tell yourself, "I do not deserve to imprison myself. I committed no crimes against society. Instead, I will accept myself."

Goal Builder 11. *Tranquillity*

Tranquillity with two 1's (remember?), because you need it so much.

Close your eyes, but this time make use of another vital organ, your ears.

Listen, and hear sounds that will bring you a sense of tranquillity. This is individual; we all have our unique tastes. Use your imagination, and listen.

Some people love to hear the sound of rain falling on city streets.

Others like to hear the roar of the ocean pounding on the shore.

Many people respond to beautiful music. For this, of course, you do not need your imagination; you can play your favorite phonograph records or listen to the radio.

Soothe yourself with the sounds you love to hear. You owe yourself this relief from life's struggles, so often full of discordant noises.

Now open your eyes, and walk to the mirror. On it write: TRANQUILLITY. Tell yourself, "I will be tranquil today. No matter how discordant the world and its problems, I will give myself tranquillity."

Goal Builder 12. *No Retirement Clock*

Once again, you listen. To the ticking of a clock. If you have a clock that ticks, use it. If not, imagine the ticking.

Time is ticking away, and time is precious. Time is ticking away, time that comprises your life, and this is your great gift.

Walk to the mirror now and write: CLOCK. Tell yourself: "I must not use this valuable time to retire from life. I must not resort to 'killing' time. My life is for translating constructive thinking and constructive imaging into constructive action."

This is what creative psycho-cybernetics means.

Goal Builder 13. *Integrity*

The person with integrity is whole, honest, honorable. He feels self-respect.

Do you feel that you cannot qualify?

Your life is a potpourri of failures?

You are unreliable?

You have lived uselessly, disconnectedly, irresponsibly?

Are you sure?

Take out paper and pencil. Close your eyes and roam through your life, connecting it up. Think of your proud moments, see them in your mind. Then write them down on paper. Draw up a list of your moments of integrity. Forgive and forget your mistakes and your irresponsibilities. Bring back your shining experiences; then list them.

And your qualities of integrity, list them too. Perhaps they are not absolute, but just because you were irresponsible in a minor way three or four times in your life, does this make you an irresponsible person or a responsible person? A responsible person, I would say, and a person with integrity. List this quality: RESPONSIBILITY. Draw up a list that gives you a fair shake.

Then read your lists, and reread them later. If you are a person of reasonable integrity, see yourself this way; don't let your perfectionism take away your right to see yourself as a person of integrity so that you frustrate your need to respect yourself.

Then walk to the mirror and write: INTEGRITY.

And say to yourself: "First, I shall look at myself with kind eyes. Second, I shall see myself at my best, as a person of confidence, rather than at my worst, as a person of frustration. Third, I forgive myself for the mistakes of yesterday. Fourth, I forgive others. Only then will integrity be a living thing for me. Only then will self-respect be a living thing for me."

Goal Builder 14. *Survival*

Survival with self-respect. In a world of uncertainty this is quite a chore!

Another movie—in your mind. You are scheduled to deliver a speech to a huge crowd of people. Workmen have been enlarging the stadium in which you are to speak so that 125,000 people will come to hear you if it doesn't rain. You can't imagine looking at such a crowd of people? I can't either. You are so nervous that when you look at yourself in the mirror you can't recognize yourself. You even forget your name. How will you survive with self-respect? You pray for rain, but the weather is ideal. Who is that stranger telling you it's time to get dressed so you can take a cab to the stadium? Oh, it's your wife (or husband)! Hurriedly, you brush your teeth with soap and wash your face with toothpaste.

You check yourself. Thank God, you have a shoe on each

foot and you're wearing clothes. But your hysteria mounts to superterror when you think of 250,000 eyes watching you as you speak. How will you survive with self-respect?

Okay, you've got the picture. Obviously it's a caricature. I am a veteran lecturer and this picture scares me, too. The question remains: How to survive?

Go to the mirror and write: SURVIVAL. Look at yourself, and tell yourself this: "I will accept my fear. And my nervousness. And my panic. My key to survival with self-respect is this: I will accept myself no matter what all these people think of me. I will stop expecting myself to be a superman. No matter how imperfect I am, I will accept myself."

How else can a person deal with such an imagined crisis? Bring images of your past successes into your mind. This will serve a dual purpose: it will encourage your success feelings to surface and replace your nervousness; second, if you make a terrible speech, these past successes will make acceptance of this failure easier for you.

Then do your best, knowing this will help you to survive such a crisis experience with self-respect. Do your best in reality, too.

Your Lifelong Goal

I hope that these exercises help you move toward self-respect. Many of them—such as the last one which involves such a dramatic situation—are purposely exaggerated and unreal so that when you come back to earth you can cope with your more common problems still more effectively.

Our tools are invisible, but extremely potent: understanding, forgiveness, success imaging, confidence building, goal orientation, and emotional readiness for constructive action.

In this chapter, as in this book, we have applied creative psycho-cybernetics to forward our search for self-respect.

Temporarily, our search is over.

But self-respect is a lifelong goal. It is one of our basic human values. If you own a plant and love it, you keep watering it as long as it lives.

Walk over to your mirror now and say this: "As long as I live, I will strive to make myself a complete person, in my own image, with a sense of mature responsibility, rising above my human limitations to realize—in good faith and with constructive intentions toward other people—my full potential for self-respect."